Manifestation – The DREAM Method in 5 Steps
Copyright © 2025 by Dr. Constance Santego.

Copy Editor & Interior Design: Constance Santego
Book Layout: ©2017 BookDesignTemplates.com

Ordering Information:
Quantity sales. Special discounts are available on quantity purchases by corporations, associations, and others. For details, contact the "Special Sales Department" at the address above.

Trade Paperback ISBN: 978-1-990062-85-8
eBook ISBN 978-1-990062-86-5
Created and published In Canada. Printed and bound in the United States of America

First Edition
Published by Maximillian Enterprises
Kelowna, BC
Canada
www.constancesantego.ca

Manifestation – The DREAM Method In 5 Steps

...TO CREATE THE LIFE YOU DREAM OF

Dr. Constance Santego

Maximillian Enterprises
Kelowna, BC

Dedication

To the dreamers,
who dare to believe in more than what they see.

To the seekers,
who know there is wisdom in both Spirit and science.

And to every soul who has ever whispered a wish to the
universe,
this book is for you.

May you remember that manifestation is not magic—it is your
birthright.
Live the DREAM, and create the life you were meant to live.

— Dr. Constance Santego

All our dreams can come true if we
have the courage to pursue them.

Walt Disney

ALSO BY DR. CONSTANCE SANTEGO

NOVELS

Illegitimate Grace
Ashcroft Hollow

Okanagan Trilogy:
Beneath the Vineyards
Under the Okanagan Sun
Guardian of the Lake

The Nine Spiritual Gifts Series:
Journey of a Soul – (Vol 1 Michael)
Language of a Soul – (Vol 2 Gabriel)
Prophecy of a Soul – (Vol 3 Bath Kol)
Healing of a Soul – (Vol 4 Raphael)
Miracles of a Soul – (Vol 5 Hamied)
Knowledge of a Soul – (Vol 6 Raziel)
Wisdom of a Soul – (Vol 7 Uriel)
Faith of a Soul – (Vol 8 Pistis Sophia)

NONFICTION
The Intuitive Life, The Gift Of Prophecy, Third Edition
Fairy Tales, Dreams And Reality... Where Are You On Your Path?
Second Edition
Your Persona... The Mask You Wear
Archangel Michael's Soul Retrieval Guide
Tesla And The Future Of Energy Medicine
Beyond Tesla: Advancing The Science Of Energy Healing
Tesla's Code: Mastering Energy, Frequency, And Creative Power
Beyond The Mind: Harnessing The Power Of Astral Projection For
Creative Awakening
Bend, Don't Break: Finding Your Way Back To Abundance
Ring Therapy: A Guide To Healing And Balance
Ring Therapy Pocket Guide
Floraopathy™: The Art And Science Of Vibrational Healing With
Essential Oils
Dear Older Me: A Memoir... Of Sorts
It's Just Like Poker: A Spiritual Guide To Playing The
Cards Life Deals You
Signs And Meanings: What The Feet Reveal About Health, Stress,
And The Body's Story
Auricions: Unlocking Subconscious Healing Through Quantum
Medicine
Quick Fix Acupressure Method

Type 3 Diabetes: *The Hidden Link Between Blood Sugar, Brain Health, and Healing Naturally*
How to Stay in Your Power Without Becoming a Narcissist (Vol 2)

REIKI WISDOM, SERIES:
Angelic Lifestyle, a Vibrant Lifestyle
Angelic Lifestyle 42-Day Energy Cleanse
Reiki and the Power of The Joint Points: Unlocking Energy Pathways for Healing (Vol I)
Reiki and Karmic Healing: Releasing Patterns From Past Lives (Vol II)
Reiki and the Five Elements (Vol III)
Secrets of a Healer, Magic Of Reiki
The Reiki Master's Manual

SECRETS OF A HEALER, SERIES:
Magic Of Aromatherapy (Vol I)
Magic Of Reflexology (Vol II)
Magic Of The Gifts (Vol III)
Magic Of Muscle Testing (Vol IV)
Magic Of Iridology (Vol V)
Magic Of Massage (Vol VI)
Magic Of Hypnotherapy (Vol VII)
Magic Of Reiki (Vol VIII)
Magic Of Advanced Aromatherapy (Vol IX)
Magic Of Esthetics (Vol X)
The Reiki Master's Manual (Vol XI)

ADULT COLORING JOURNALS
SERIES-ZEN COLORING:
Quantum Energy and Mindful Living Journal (Vol 1)
Reiki Energy Journal (Vol 2)
Nine Spiritual Gifts Journal (Vol 3)
I Forgive Journal (Vol 4)

FOR CHILDREN
I am Big Tonight. I Don't Need the Light

COOKBOOK
My Favorite Recipes, with a Hint of Giggle

BUISNESS
How To Use ChatGPT For Authors: From Idea To Published Book
Scaling Beyond 6 Figures: Strategies For Health & Wellness Professionals
The Academypreneur's Playbook: Turn Knowledge Into A Revenue-Generating School

HUMOR/GIFT BOOK
How Do You Like Your Eggs? *Crack Into Your Personality, Yolk and All*

Contents

Preface

For as long as I can remember, people have spoken of manifestation as if it were something magical, mysterious, or reserved for the few who somehow "figured it out." I have witnessed both students and clients struggle with the process — excited at the thought of creating a new reality, but frustrated when their results felt inconsistent or fleeting.

Over the years, through my own study, teaching, and lived experience, I began to notice a pattern. Manifestation wasn't random at all. It followed a rhythm, a cycle, a set of natural stages that could be recognized, repeated, and refined. What was often missing in most teachings was *clarity* and *structure*.

That realization inspired me to create **The DREAM Method**: a simple, five-step process that makes manifestation practical, grounded, and accessible to everyone. Each step — Drift, Recognize, Execute, Achieve, and Master — corresponds to a part of the journey from unconscious thought to realized experience. The final step, Master, emphasizes reflection, because manifestation isn't just about "getting" what you want; it's about growing into who you are meant to become.

This book is both a guide and an invitation. A guide, because it gives you the tools and exercises to follow the method in your daily life. An invitation, because it asks you to partner with Spirit, to take responsibility for your thoughts and actions, and to step fully into your role as creator of your own life.

My hope is that, as you read these pages, you will discover that manifestation is not magic — it is a method. And that method can change everything.

Note to Reader

This book is not meant to be read passively and placed back on the shelf. *The DREAM Method* is a practice — a way of thinking, acting, and reflecting that becomes more powerful the more you use it.

As you move through each chapter, you'll find explanations, examples, and exercises designed to help you apply the steps to your own life. Take your time. Pause when something resonates. Journal your experiences. Try the exercises more than once. Each time you do, you'll notice deeper insights and greater alignment.

Remember, manifestation is not instant gratification. It is a cycle. Sometimes the results come quickly, like finding a pen when you need one. Other times, it unfolds over weeks, months, or even years, like building a career, creating a family, or living your soul's calling.

Trust the process. Celebrate the small manifestations as much as the big ones. And know that even when the outcome looks different than you expected, Spirit is guiding you toward your highest good.

This is your journey. Read with an open mind, practice with an open heart, and allow yourself to *live the DREAM.*

— Dr. Constance Santego

WHAT I MEAN BY "SPIRIT"

Throughout this book, you'll see me use the word *Spirit.*
I use it in a broad, inclusive way — not tied to any one religion or belief system.

Spirit is the invisible force that connects life together. Some may call it God, Source, the Universe, Higher Self, Divine Intelligence, or even simply *the energy of possibility.* Others may think of it as their own subconscious mind, the field of collective thought, or the mystery of nature.

Whatever name resonates with you is welcome here. For the purpose of this book, Spirit simply means:

The greater intelligence that responds to and supports the unfolding of your thoughts, actions, and intentions.

You don't have to believe in anything supernatural to use the DREAM Method. You only need to be open to the idea that your mind is powerful, your choices matter, and life has a way of responding to both.

How to Use This Book

Manifestation – The DREAM Method in 5 Steps is designed to be both a guide and a companion. It's not just something to read once; it's a process you can return to again and again as your desires, goals, and life evolve.

Here's how to get the most from it:

1. **Read in Order**
   The steps build on each other: Drift → Recognize → Execute → Achieve → Master. Reading in sequence will help you understand how each stage flows into the next.
2. **Pause for Reflection**
   Throughout the book, you'll find exercises, journaling prompts, and meditations. Don't skip them. These are the tools that turn knowledge into experience.
3. **Practice Consistently**
   The DREAM Method is most effective when used daily — even in small ways. Try applying it to simple desires (like finding a parking spot) as well as to bigger goals.
4. **Use a Journal**
   Keep a dedicated notebook or journal as you work through the steps. Writing clarifies your thoughts and helps you recognize patterns in your manifestations.
5. **Trust Your Timing**
   Some manifestations are quick, others take time. Don't judge your progress by speed alone. Every step, including reflection, is part of your alignment with Spirit and your true self.
6. **Return Often**
   This is not a "one and done" method. Each time you

revisit the process, you'll uncover new insights and refine your ability to manifest with clarity and confidence.

Tip: The final chapter includes integration practices to help you weave the DREAM Method into your everyday life. Think of this book as a cycle, not a straight line — each manifestation prepares you for the next.

Throughout this book, you'll find invitations to join me on YouTube, where I've created short videos that guide you through each of the five DREAM steps. These videos are designed to complement what you're reading — giving you a chance to practice, reflect, and embody the teachings with me.

Manifestation – The DREAM Method In 5 Steps

...TO CREATE THE LIFE YOU DREAM OF

Live the DREAM: Drift, Recognize, Execute, Achieve, Master.

Dr. Constance Santego

Introduction: The Power of the DREAM Method

For centuries, people have spoken about the power of manifestation — the ability to bring thoughts, desires, and dreams into reality. Countless books, workshops, and teachings have promised the "secret" to making it happen. And yet, for many, manifestation still feels mysterious, inconsistent, or even disappointing.

Why?

Because most approaches only tell part of the story. They might encourage you to visualize, to affirm, or to "think positive" — but they often overlook the deeper mechanics of how thoughts form, how they gain momentum, and what happens once the manifestation appears. Without understanding the *whole* cycle, it's easy to feel like manifestation is a hit-or-miss game — a lucky accident rather than a repeatable practice.

The truth is simple: manifestation isn't magic, and it isn't random. It follows a natural sequence — from unconscious spark, to conscious intention, to aligned action, to lived experience, and finally to reflection. Once you understand this sequence, you can work with it deliberately instead of stumbling through it unconsciously.

That is what **The DREAM Method** is all about.

It's not just another way of talking about wishful thinking. It's a grounded, 5-step method that takes you from a fleeting thought to a realized experience — and then shows you how to master the cycle so you can create again and again, with greater clarity and alignment each time.

When you learn to *Live the DREAM — Drift, Recognize, Execute, Achieve, Master* — manifestation stops being mysterious. It becomes practical. Predictable. Aligned. And most importantly, it becomes yours to use: not as a fleeting trick, but as an ongoing art and science of creation.

HOW THE DREAM METHOD DEMYSTIFIES MANIFESTATION

Manifestation often feels confusing because it's usually presented as an abstract idea: "Just think positive" or "Ask, believe, receive." While these phrases inspire, they rarely explain how thoughts actually become reality — or why sometimes they don't.

The DREAM Method removes the guesswork by breaking manifestation into five clear, practical stages. Instead of leaving you wondering if you're "doing it right," this method gives you a map — a step-by-step cycle from the first spark of thought to the moment it blossoms into lived experience.

Each stage builds on the last:

1. **Drift** – A thought emerges unconsciously.
2. **Recognize** – You bring it into conscious focus.
3. **Execute** – You begin aligning with it through energy and action.
4. **Achieve** – The manifestation itself takes form.
5. **Master** – Reflection allows you to refine, evolve, or begin the cycle anew.

By seeing manifestation as a process instead of a mystery, you gain clarity. You realize that nothing appears "out of nowhere."

Every reality you experience begins with a thought, grows through awareness, takes shape through action, and continues — or dissolves — based on what you learn from it.

This is how the DREAM Method transforms manifestation from a vague hope into a reliable practice — a cycle you can understand, track, and refine.

THE PROMISE OF THE DREAM METHOD

Manifestation is not a special gift reserved for a chosen few. It is a natural process that every human being is already using — consciously or not. Every experience in your life began as a thought: some unconscious, some intentional, many repeated until they became strong enough to shape your choices and create your reality.

The difference between those who manifest with intention and those who feel powerless in their lives is simple: awareness.

When you understand how thoughts drift into your mind, how they can be recognized, executed, achieved, and mastered, you gain the ability to direct the process instead of being swept along by it. You stop questioning whether manifestation works and begin to see how it is *always* working — in your relationships, your health, your finances, your growth.

The promise of the DREAM Method is this: once you learn to guide the stages of thought, energy, and reflection, manifestation will no longer feel like chance. It will become practical, teachable, and repeatable. And most importantly, it will become something you can do every day, to create the life you dream of.

Chapter 1 – Drift: Unconscious Thought

Theme: Seeds are planted before we even notice.

D – Drift
(Unconscious Thought: the spark, the first glimpse)
Every manifestation begins as a passing drift of thought. These "drift-thoughts" float through the mind almost unnoticed — subtle, fleeting, yet full of potential. Or you might like to think of it this way: every manifestation begins with a seed, and more often than not, that seed is planted without our awareness.

These are the drift-thoughts — the subtle whispers of the mind shaped by your environment, emotions, memories, and conditioning. They float through almost unnoticed — fleeting, yet full of potential. And even if you don't pay attention, Spirit always does.

Unconscious thoughts arise in everyday moments:

- A commercial flashes across the screen, and suddenly you crave something you hadn't thought of before.
- The smell of fresh bread drifts from a bakery, and your body responds before your mind has even caught up.
- A childhood memory is triggered by a song, quietly steering your mood and your choices for the rest of the day.

Psychologists estimate that more than **90% of our daily decisions** are influenced by unconscious thought. These hidden mental processes don't ask for permission; they bubble up automatically from past experiences, ingrained beliefs, and the emotions you carry.

Conditioning also plays a role. If you grew up hearing *"money doesn't grow on trees,"* unconscious thoughts about scarcity may color your choices even decades later. If you were praised for creativity, unconscious thoughts of innovation may guide you toward opportunities without you realizing why.

Unconscious thought is neither good nor bad — it is simply **the soil** from which manifestation grows. The challenge is that, unless you bring awareness to it, you may be manifesting realities rooted in fears, doubts, or outdated patterns rather than your true desires.

This is why the DREAM Method begins here. By learning to notice and work with unconscious thought, you start to recognize the seeds being planted in your mind long before they sprout into reality.

THE BRAIN AND UNCONSCIOUS THOUGHT

Unconscious thoughts are not accidents — they are shaped and filtered by powerful systems within your brain. The main region involved is the **subconscious mind**, which scientists often connect to the **limbic system** and the **basal ganglia**.

- **The Limbic System** (including the amygdala and hippocampus) stores emotional memories and triggers automatic responses. This is why a smell, sound, or song can suddenly bring a thought or memory into your mind without effort.
- **The Basal Ganglia** plays a role in habits and repetitive behaviors. It is the part of the brain that runs "on

autopilot," generating unconscious thoughts that guide routine decisions without needing your full awareness.

- **The Reticular Activating System (RAS)** acts like a filter. It decides which bits of information from your environment get your attention and which ones drift into the background. If something slips past the filter, it often enters as an unconscious thought.

Together, these systems act like a **background processor**. They keep scanning your environment, emotions, and stored memories, generating thoughts before you're even aware of them.

From a spiritual perspective, you might say the brain provides the *hardware*, while Spirit provides the *signal*. Your unconscious thoughts are the sparks created where biology and spirit meet — tiny nudges that show you what's possible.

Key Insight: The unconscious mind is always active. You don't have to "try" to generate thoughts; they arise naturally from the way your brain is wired. The choice — and the art of manifestation — begins when you decide which of those thoughts to bring into conscious focus.

THE PSYCHOLOGY OF PRIMING

Why random thoughts are never fully random.

What may feel like a random thought is often the result of a powerful psychological effect known as **priming**. Priming happens when exposure to one stimulus influences how we think, feel, or behave in the moments that follow — usually without us realizing it.

For example:

- If you see the color yellow and then someone asks you to name a fruit, you're more likely to say "banana" than "apple."
- If you hear words related to kindness before meeting someone, you're more likely to approach them with warmth and trust.
- Advertisers use this constantly: showing images of luxury, health, or happiness to prime you toward wanting their product.

Priming works because your unconscious mind is always scanning and absorbing information, linking it to memories and emotional associations. These links then quietly influence your next thoughts and actions.

This is why "random" ideas appear in your mind. They are rarely random at all — they are the result of countless subtle cues: what you saw, heard, smelled, felt, or even remembered a few minutes ago.

In terms of manifestation, priming matters because it sets the stage. If your environment is filled with negativity, your unconscious thoughts will often reflect worry, fear, or limitation. If your environment is filled with inspiration, gratitude, and possibility, your unconscious mind will more likely feed you thoughts aligned with growth and opportunity.

Key Insight: The thoughts that drift into your mind are not accidents — they are responses to the cues and conditions around you. By becoming aware of priming, you begin to see how your inner world and outer environment are already shaping your manifestations long before you make a conscious choice.

EVERYDAY EXAMPLES OF UNCONSCIOUS THOUGHT

Unconscious thought shows up in the smallest moments of daily life — often so quickly that we miss the link between stimulus and response.

- **Feeling Thirsty:** On a hot afternoon, your body signals discomfort without consciously deciding; a thought about cold water or a refreshing drink flashes through your mind. The heat primed the thought, and thirst shaped it into desire.
- **Sudden Craving:** You weren't hungry a moment ago, but the smell of coffee, bread, or popcorn in the air immediately awakens a craving. Your unconscious has been triggered by sensory input.
- **Overhearing an Idea:** Someone nearby mentions a vacation destination or a business idea. Hours later, the thought is still echoing in your mind, nudging you to research flights or sketch out plans. The seed was planted simply by overhearing a few words.
- **Emotional Echo:** A song plays on the radio, and without effort, you're transported back to a memory. The emotional state linked to that memory influences your mood, decisions, and even the thoughts that follow.

These examples remind us that the unconscious mind is always active, collecting cues from the environment and weaving them into new thoughts. What seems spontaneous is often a chain reaction you didn't notice beginning.

DREAMS AND THE SUBCONSCIOUS

One of the most powerful ways unconscious thoughts reveal themselves is through nighttime dreams. When you sleep, your conscious defenses are lowered. The part of your mind that usually filters, organizes, or dismisses thoughts grows quiet. What rises instead is your subconscious — speaking in images, emotions, and stories.

These dreams often reflect **drift-thoughts**: the subtle seeds of desire, fear, or memory that have been planted without your awareness. In dreams, they may appear as symbols, metaphors, or vivid experiences that feel real in the moment. A dream about being trapped might point to a hidden belief about limitation. A dream of flying might reveal a longing for freedom.

Science of Dreams

From a psychological perspective, dreams are how the brain processes memory, emotion, and unresolved experiences. During REM sleep, neurons fire in ways that mimic waking life, but without the same logic or control. The result is a dreamscape where unconscious material surfaces. Freud called dreams "the royal road to the unconscious," while modern neuroscience views them as a kind of emotional and cognitive rehearsal.

Spirit in Dreams

Spirit also speaks through dreams. Many spiritual traditions treat dreams as sacred messages — guiding, warning, or inspiring the dreamer. In the Bible, Joseph received guidance through dreams. In Indigenous teachings, dreams are honored as communication from ancestors. In energy medicine, dreams are often seen as the soul's way of working through lessons.

Whether you view dreams psychologically, spiritually, or both, they are a powerful bridge to Drift.

Why Pay Attention

Sometimes dreams are random fragments of the day — your mind sorting through details. But often, they carry deeper meaning. A recurring dream, especially one that feels emotionally charged, may be a signal that your subconscious is trying to show you where attention is needed. Ignoring it can keep the drift-thought hidden; recognizing it gives you the chance to nurture or release it.

Practice: Dream Journaling

Keeping a dream journal helps bring the unconscious into consciousness. Place a notebook beside your bed and write down any dreams you recall immediately upon waking. Don't worry if they don't make sense. Over time, patterns will emerge:

- What images repeat?
- What emotions surface most often?
- Do certain dreams align with desires you are trying to manifest?
- Are there fears showing up that might sabotage your process?

By honoring your dreams as part of the **Drift** stage, you begin to see how deeply connected your inner and outer worlds really are. Every dream is either a mirror of what is already within you or a whisper of what Spirit is guiding you toward.

USING DREAM JOURNALING TO UNCOVER HIDDEN DESIRES OR BLOCKS

Dream journaling is more than simply recording what you remember at night — it is a way of listening to your subconscious. Often, your deepest desires and your most stubborn blocks are revealed in dreams long before you notice them in waking life.

For example, you may dream repeatedly of traveling or exploring new places. On the surface, it looks like a simple story. But underneath, it may point to a hidden desire for freedom, expansion, or change. Likewise, if you dream of being chased, stuck, or unprepared, your subconscious may be revealing fears or limiting beliefs that are blocking your ability to move forward.

By writing these dreams down, you create a record that allows you to step back and see the patterns. Over time, you may notice that the same themes, symbols, or feelings reappear. These are valuable clues:

- **Desires** show up as dreams of opportunities, adventures, love, or success.
- **Blocks** often appear as fears, frustrations, failures, or obstacles.

When you pay attention to both, you gain insight into what is quietly shaping your manifestations. You may discover that Spirit is planting seeds of guidance, urging you to recognize what you truly want — and to clear away what no longer serves you.

LUCID DREAMING AS A TOOL FOR CONSCIOUS RECOGNITION

Lucid dreaming occurs when you become aware that you are dreaming while still inside the dream. In this state, the boundaries between Drift (unconscious thought) and Recognize (conscious thought) blur. You are awake within your own subconscious.

Why is this powerful for manifestation? Because lucid dreaming allows you to **practice recognition in real time**. Instead of passively watching your dream unfold, you can:

- Notice the thoughts, images, or symbols as they appear.
- Ask yourself: *"What does this represent? What is this trying to show me?"*
- Experiment with shifting the dream — choosing a different action, opening a door, flying instead of running, embracing instead of fighting.

Every choice you make in a lucid dream trains your brain to recognize and redirect unconscious drift-thoughts. You are literally rehearsing conscious creation in your sleep.

Some people use lucid dreaming to visualize a goal, meet with guides, or dissolve recurring nightmares. Others simply use it as a way to strengthen their sense of agency. No matter how you approach it, lucid dreaming is a reminder that you are never powerless — even in your dreams, you can learn to choose.

THE WAY SPIRIT CAN COMMUNICATE THROUGH DREAMS

Dreams are more than the mind's way of processing memory and emotion. Across cultures and traditions, they have also been honored as a sacred channel of Spirit. When the conscious mind quiets during sleep, you become more receptive to guidance that might otherwise go unnoticed.

Spirit can use dreams to:

- **Offer guidance:** A dream may present a symbol, mentor, or path that clarifies your next step.
- **Deliver warnings:** Nightmares sometimes serve as alerts, showing you what needs attention or what to avoid.
- **Provide comfort:** Dreams of departed loved ones can bring reassurance that you are not alone.
- **Confirm alignment:** Recurring dreams of joy, freedom, or fulfillment may signal that you are moving in harmony with Spirit's support.

In this way, dreams act like signposts along your manifestation journey. They don't always provide direct answers, but they often illuminate the energy surrounding your desires — whether supportive or resistant.

When you wake from a dream that feels especially vivid, emotional, or symbolic, pause to ask:
"What is Spirit showing me here?"
Even if the meaning isn't immediately clear, trust that Spirit's language often comes through feelings, impressions, or repeated imagery rather than literal instruction.

By welcoming dreams as a form of spiritual dialogue, you honor Drift not just as unconscious thought, but as sacred communication — an invitation to co-create with Spirit at the deepest level.

BEDTIME INTENTION PRACTICE

The last thoughts you hold before falling asleep often shape both your dreams and the unconscious seeds you plant. By setting an intention at night, you invite Spirit to guide you through rest, dreams, and into manifestation.

Before sleep, try saying one of these aloud or silently to yourself:

- *"I welcome clarity, healing, and inspiration in my dreams. May they show me the seeds I am ready to grow."*
- *"As I drift into sleep, I plant thoughts of love, abundance, and joy. Spirit, help me nurture them."*
- *"I release the day and open myself to divine guidance. My dreams align me with what serves my highest good."*
- *"Spirit, guide my dreams tonight. Reveal what I need to see, hear, or know for my highest good."*

You can also make your own affirmation by blending three parts:

1. **Release** – letting go of the day.
2. **Request** – asking for guidance or clarity.
3. **Receive** – affirming openness to what comes.

As you fall asleep, imagine your words sinking into the fertile soil of your subconscious — seeds waiting to grow into tomorrow's manifestations.

STORY EXAMPLE –
STEP 1: DRIFT—UNCONSCIOUS THOUGHT

Imagine you are working outside on a hot summer day. The sun is beating down, your skin is warm, and sweat trickles along your brow. In that moment, a thought flickers across your mind: *"Swimming would feel amazing right now."*

The thought comes and goes in an instant. You don't pause to consider it. You don't start planning for it. You simply return to what you were doing, and the idea of swimming dissolves as quickly as it appeared.

This is the nature of **unconscious thought**. It is a spark — a suggestion of possibility — but without your attention, it remains only that. Spirit hears it, but Spirit does not act. The thought has not been chosen, repeated, or energized, so it does not take root.

Unconscious thoughts like this pass through your mind countless times each day. Most never become anything more. They are the first stage of manifestation, but only when you decide to notice and nurture them do they begin to grow into reality.

SPIRITUAL PERSPECTIVE EXAMPLE – STEP 1: DRIFT—UNCONSCIOUS THOUGHT

Unconscious thoughts are quick, fleeting sparks of awareness that pass through your mind without weight or attachment. They come and go in a split second — often so lightly that you dismiss them as unimportant.

Imagine this: you're at work, completely absorbed in your tasks. Out of nowhere, a thought pops into your mind: *"Mexico."* You see yourself there for just a moment, but then the thought vanishes as quickly as it came. You don't dwell on it. You don't give it meaning. You move on.

From a spiritual perspective, Spirit hears *every single one* of these unconscious thoughts. Millions of them are floating through the mind at any given moment, and Spirit receives them all. But because they are fleeting and unfocused, Spirit pays no attention to them. They are background noise — sparks without fuel.

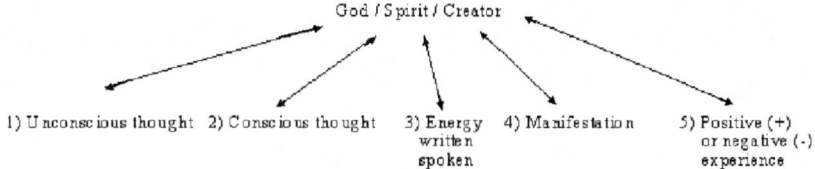

This is why not every passing thought becomes a reality. Spirit does not respond to every unconscious impulse because you, the creator, have not claimed it. You haven't given it enough energy, repetition, or intention for it to be taken seriously.

Think of unconscious thought as the **raw material of creation**. It's like planting a seed in soil without watering it. Spirit notes its presence, but until you nurture it, it will not grow.

Key Insight: The unconscious stage is where manifestation always begins, but without attention, it ends as quickly as it starts. Spirit is listening, but Spirit is waiting for you to decide what matters.

PERSONAL STORY: TRUSTING THE DRIFT

Many years ago, while I was taking a course on psychic development, my group and I traveled to Vernon, BC, to attend a mediumship demonstration. Halfway there, we received word that the presentation had been cancelled. Our bus turned around, and along the way, we happened to notice a psychic fair being advertised. Since we suddenly had free time, we decided to stop in.

Some members of our group went for readings, others wandered the booths. I was drawn to a table where a man was selling used books. Without thinking, I said to him, *"You have the book Holy Blood, Holy Grail."*

He looked at me and replied, *"No, I don't."*

I said again, *"Yes, you do."*

At this point, two of my classmates joined me at the table. They gently reminded me, *"Connie, he said no."* I just shrugged and repeated, *"Well, he does."* Then I turned away to browse elsewhere, brushing off the moment.

A minute later, I noticed the man lift the tablecloth, reach underneath, and pull out a book. He turned toward me and said, *"You mean this book?"* And there it was — *Holy Blood, Holy Grail.*

I couldn't help but smile and simply reply, *"I told you, you had it."* Naturally, I bought the book.

The Lesson

Looking back, this was a clear example of the **Drift step.** A thought surfaced quickly and strongly — I knew the book was there, even when everyone else insisted it wasn't. My conscious mind might have doubted it, but Spirit had already whispered the truth.

Moments like these remind us that **Spirit hears the drift-thoughts we often dismiss.** If we learn to trust them — instead of brushing them away — they can lead us straight to what we're seeking.

TIP & WARNING: THE SHADOW SIDE OF UNCONSCIOUS THOUGHT

Unconscious thoughts are powerful because they operate beneath the surface, but this power can work **for** you or **against** you. Just as your unconscious mind plants seeds of inspiration and desire, it can also plant seeds of limitation.

These often show up as **limiting beliefs** — thoughts formed long ago through conditioning, fear, or painful experiences. For example:

- *"I'm not good enough."*
- *"Money is hard to come by."*
- *"Love always ends in heartbreak."*

Left unchecked, these unconscious patterns can sabotage your manifestations. Instead of attracting opportunities, you may unconsciously filter them out. Instead of moving forward, you may sabotage your own progress without realizing why.

Tip: The key is awareness. When you notice recurring negative thoughts, write them down. Then gently question them: *Is this belief really true? Is it mine, or was it planted by someone else? Does it still serve me?*

Warning: If you ignore limiting beliefs, they will continue to manifest situations that confirm them. Your outer reality will mirror the inner script you've left unchallenged.

The good news is this: once an unconscious thought becomes conscious, you have the power to reshape it. Awareness is the first step to freedom.

COMMON PITFALLS

- Ignoring fleeting thoughts that could be seeds of true desire.
- Letting negative unconscious patterns (fear, worry, self-doubt) run unchecked.
- Believing random thoughts "don't matter" — when in truth, Spirit hears them all.

EXERCISE: JOURNALING YOUR UNCONSCIOUS SEEDS

To begin working with unconscious thought, you first need to notice it. For one week, keep a small notebook or use the notes app on your phone to track the thoughts that "just pop up" throughout your day. Don't judge them, and don't try to make sense of them — simply write them down.

Daily Prompts:

1. What spontaneous thoughts did I notice today?
2. Did any of these thoughts come after something I saw, heard, smelled, or felt?
3. Which thoughts kept recurring throughout the day or week?
4. Did I take any action, even small, because of these thoughts?
5. Looking back, which of these might be early seeds of manifestation?

Example entry:

- *Random thought: "I'd love to go swimming." Noticed it twice today — once when I saw kids with towels, once when I felt overheated in the car. Later, I checked local pool schedules. Seed planted!*

Reflection at the end of the week:

- Circle the recurring thoughts.
- Ask: *Do these align with what I truly want to manifest, or are they habits and distractions planted by outside influences?*

By journaling, you'll start to see how unconscious thought isn't random at all — it's a fertile field, and some of the seeds planted there are worth nurturing into reality.

WANT TO GO DEEPER?

If you'd like a guided experience of this step, I've created a companion video for you on my YouTube channel. In it, I walk you through the process of **STEP 1: Drift-Unconscious Thought** so you can practice it in real time.

You can watch it here:
https://youtu.be/hSxlyzlwYtg
and/or
https://youtu.be/Mv2f6GwXFLY

Chapter 2 – Recognize: Conscious Thought

Theme: Awareness and intention transform the seed.

R – Recognize (bringing unconscious into consciousness)
When you choose to notice and hold a thought, you bring it into focus. Recognition turns random sparks into intentional seeds. This is where you clarify and commit.

In Step 1, unconscious thought drifts in and out of your mind like passing clouds. It is unclaimed, fleeting, and often forgotten. But the moment you pause, notice, and give a thought your attention, it shifts into something far more powerful — it becomes a **conscious thought**.

This is the turning point in manifestation. The seed that once lay dormant begins to take root.

A **random thought** is like a whisper you ignore, but a **chosen thought** is one you recognize, revisit, and begin to shape. The shift happens when you say to yourself, *"Yes, this matters. I want to think more about this."*

For example, you briefly thought of swimming on a hot day. Later, while talking with a friend about weekend plans, the thought surfaces again, and this time you imagine what it would feel like to dive into cool water. You're not just experiencing a passing impulse — you're actively giving attention to it, picturing details, and holding it in your awareness.

This is where intention is born. You may not yet be taking action, but you are **choosing** to return to the thought, adding clarity and emotional charge. Spirit hears the difference. Unlike the millions of unconscious sparks that fade away, a conscious thought rings louder, clearer, and stronger in the field of creation.

Key Insight: Conscious thought is the bridge between possibility and potential. It is the moment you decide which seeds are worth nurturing into reality.

THE BRAIN AND CONSCIOUS THOUGHT

When a thought shifts from unconscious to conscious, different areas of the brain become active, conscious thought is no longer automatic; it requires awareness, focus, and often imagination.

- **The Prefrontal Cortex**: This is the "thinking brain." It helps you focus, plan, and set goals. When you consciously choose a thought, the prefrontal cortex is engaged, turning a vague idea into something deliberate.
- **The Hippocampus**: This region works with memory. It allows you to recall past experiences and use them to build a detailed picture of what you're thinking about now.
- **The Reticular Activating System (RAS)**: This filtering system, which already influences unconscious thought, now sharpens its focus. Once you consciously decide a thought matters — like going to Mexico or buying a new home — the RAS begins noticing opportunities, conversations, and information that match it.

From a spiritual perspective, conscious thought is like shining a spotlight on one seed among millions. Your brain is now feeding it attention, energy, and imagination, while Spirit begins to notice the consistency of your focus.

Key Insight: Conscious thought isn't just "thinking harder." It's the deliberate act of choosing what to pay attention to. The brain responds by engaging higher functions of focus and planning, while Spirit responds by amplifying the thought in the energetic field of creation.

NEUROSCIENCE: NEURONS THAT FIRE TOGETHER, WIRE TOGETHER

One of the most important discoveries in neuroscience is the principle often summed up as:
"Neurons that fire together, wire together."

This means that every time you think a thought, specific neural pathways in your brain are activated. If you return to that thought repeatedly — through visualization, affirmations, or simply dwelling on it — those neurons fire in the same pattern again and again. Over time, the pathway becomes stronger, faster, and easier to access.

Think of it like walking through tall grass: the first time you step through, the path is faint and quickly disappears. But if you walk the same way every day, the grass flattens, the soil hardens, and soon you have a well-trodden trail. Your brain works the same way. Conscious thought, repeated with intention, becomes a mental pathway that feels natural and automatic.

From a manifestation perspective, this is crucial. When you consciously hold a vision of your desire, your brain is literally rewiring itself to make that thought more familiar, believable, and attainable. The more the pathway strengthens, the more your brain — and your actions — align with it.

Spirit responds to this consistency too. A thought repeated with focus and belief gains vibrational strength. The brain builds the pathway, and Spirit carries the signal, creating a partnership between biology and energy.

Key Insight: Conscious manifestation isn't just "wishful thinking." It's a neurological process of rewiring your brain to support the reality you want — and a spiritual process of aligning your energy with what you choose to create.

THE POWER OF VISUALIZATION, AFFIRMATIONS, AND REPETITION

Once a thought becomes conscious, the way you hold and nurture it determines whether it fades away or grows into reality. Three simple but powerful tools strengthen conscious thought: **visualization, affirmations, and repetition.**

- **Visualization**
  The brain cannot easily distinguish between what is vividly imagined and what is physically experienced. When you visualize, you create mental "rehearsals" that strengthen neural pathways as if the event were already happening. Picture yourself swimming in the cool water, feeling the splash, hearing the laughter around you. The more detailed the picture, the more real it becomes to your mind — and the more strongly Spirit hears it.
- **Affirmations**
  Words carry vibration. When you repeatedly affirm your intention out loud or in your thoughts, you are programming both your conscious and unconscious mind. Saying *"I am ready to receive joy, abundance, and peace"* is not just positive thinking — it is a signal of clarity and alignment that Spirit responds to— affirmations plant roots in the fertile ground of the subconscious, replacing old limiting beliefs with empowered truths.
- **Repetition**
  Manifestation thrives on consistency. A thought you

entertain once may not take hold, but a thought you return to daily gains strength and momentum. Repetition builds belief, and belief fuels manifestation. Spirit pays attention to what you return to again and again, knowing this is what you truly desire.

Together, these three practices transform a passing idea into a living intention. Visualization creates the inner movie, affirmations give it voice, and repetition gives it power. When aligned, they create a steady, amplified vibration that prepares the way for manifestation to move into action.

Key Insight: What you focus on grows. By practicing visualization, affirmations, and repetition, you tell both your brain and Spirit: *"This is what matters. This is what I choose to create."*

EXAMPLES OF CONSCIOUS THOUGHT

Conscious thought takes shape when you give attention to an idea and begin to imagine it in detail. What was once a fleeting spark becomes a story you return to, coloring it with emotion, imagery, and intention.

- **Daydreaming About a New Job**
  You start picturing yourself in a new role, imagining the office, your coworkers, or even the feeling of being paid more. Each time you think about it, the vision feels more possible, and your belief grows stronger.
- **Planning a Vacation**
  Instead of just brushing off a quick thought about travel, you allow yourself to visualize the location. You picture the beaches, the food, the hotel room. The more vividly you imagine it, the more likely you are to take the first step to make it real.
- **Imagining a New Relationship**
  You think about what kind of partner you'd like,

replaying conversations in your mind or picturing the way it feels to walk hand in hand. These conscious thoughts set the tone for the energy you send into the world and the kind of person you're inviting into your life.

- **Visualizing Healing**
  If you're working with wellness, you might consciously hold the thought of your body being healthy and strong. You picture your cells glowing with vitality or imagine energy flowing freely. This conscious focus influences not only your brain and body but also signals Spirit that this is a chosen desire.

In each case, what began as a simple idea becomes stronger, more detailed, and more alive. Conscious thought is the first sign that you are ready to nurture a seed into a reality.

CASE STUDY: NIKOLA TESLA AND THE POWER OF VISUALIZATION

One of the most remarkable examples of conscious thought in action comes from the brilliant inventor **Nikola Tesla**. Unlike many of his contemporaries, Tesla rarely built prototypes first. Instead, he relied on the extraordinary power of **visualization**.

Tesla described how he would picture an invention in his mind with such clarity that he could "see" it working long before he ever touched a piece of machinery. He would visualize every detail — the dimensions, the movement of parts, even the wear and tear over time. He claimed he could run these mental machines for weeks in his imagination, then return to them and notice where friction had appeared or parts had failed. By the time he built them physically, his designs were nearly flawless.

This wasn't magic — it was mastery of conscious thought. Tesla didn't let fleeting ideas slip away. He chose to focus on them, sharpen them, and replay them in his mind until they became real, tangible, and practical. His inventions, from the alternating current motor to wireless communication concepts, were born through this process.

Tesla's method demonstrates a profound truth: **when you consistently return to a conscious thought, it gains structure, clarity, and power.** The brain wires itself to believe in it, Spirit recognizes the signal, and eventually, the idea manifests in the physical world.

Lesson for You: You don't need Tesla's genius to apply this principle. Whether your vision is for a new home, a healed body, or a creative project, the act of repeatedly visualizing it in detail strengthens the pathway between thought and reality.

STORY EXAMPLE –
STEP 2: RECOGNIZE—CONSCIOUS THOUGHT

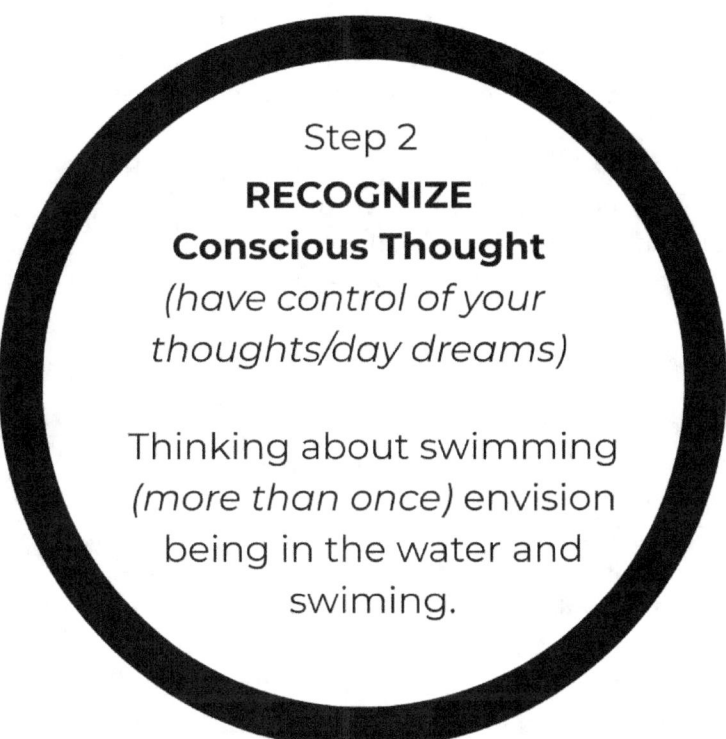

Step 2

RECOGNIZE

Conscious Thought

*(have control of your
thoughts/day dreams)*

Thinking about swimming
(more than once) envision
being in the water and
swiming.

A couple of hours later, the heat becomes almost unbearable.
The sun feels heavier, sweat runs down your back, and your
body craves relief. This time, instead of a fleeting thought, you
pause and imagine what it would be like to dive into cool water.

The picture sharpens in your mind. You don't just think
"swimming" — you think about swimming *with your friend.*
You see the two of you laughing, splashing, and cooling down
together. The idea has evolved from a brief impulse into a

conscious thought that you return to with greater clarity and emotion.

This is the moment where the seed begins to take root. You've shifted from unconscious to conscious. Spirit hears it differently now, too — not as background noise but as a focused signal. You've chosen to hold this thought, giving it energy and intention.

What was once just a passing flicker has now become something your mind and heart are starting to nurture.

SPIRITUAL PERSPECTIVE EXAMPLE – STEP 2: RECOGNIZE—CONSCIOUS THOUGHT

Conscious thought is not fleeting; it is chosen. It's the thought you return to, shaping it with more detail each time.

Imagine this: a few weeks after that first unconscious spark, a friend casually mentions that he's planning a trip to Mexico. He looks at you and asks, *"Would you like to come along?"*

This time, the thought lingers. You go home and think about it. You picture the beaches, the food, the sun. You imagine the feeling of being there, not just the word *Mexico*. The thought has grown richer, more textured, and alive with possibility.

From a spiritual perspective, this shift is profound. Spirit hears every unconscious thought, but when you return to an idea with attention and detail, Spirit begins to **pay attention to you**. It's as though your signal has grown louder, more consistent, and more deliberate.

God / Spirit / Creator

1) Unconscious thought   2) Conscious thought   3) Energy written spoken   4) Manifestation   5) Positive (+) or negative (-) experience

At this stage, your conscious thought becomes a clear message in the energetic field: *"This is something I desire. This is something I am considering with intention."* Spirit responds by opening subtle pathways — aligning opportunities, connections, and synchronicities to meet your growing vision.

Key Insight: When you choose a thought and give it focus, Spirit knows you are beginning to claim it. What was once background noise is now a meaningful request.

TIP & WARNING: THE SHADOW SIDE OF CONSCIOUS THOUGHT

Conscious thought is powerful — but like all powerful tools, it has a shadow side. When you focus on a desire with clarity and emotion, you set manifestation into motion. But if you focus with fear, worry, or doubt, you are just as effectively planting seeds you don't want.

The Shadow Side Looks Like:

- **Rumination:** Playing the same negative scenario over and over in your mind until it feels inevitable.
- **What-if Loops:** *"What if I fail? What if they leave? What if it all goes wrong?"* Each "what if" strengthens the possibility.
- **Over-attachment:** Obsessing about timing, method, or control — strangling the flow instead of trusting it.

Tip: Notice the emotional charge behind your conscious thoughts. If they leave you feeling expansive, inspired, and open, you are on the right track. If they leave you feeling tight, fearful, or heavy, shift immediately by reframing or redirecting.

Warning: Spirit does not filter "positive" from "negative." It responds to whatever vibration you hold. That's why conscious thought is a responsibility as much as a gift — what you focus on with intensity is what you invite into form.

Key Insight: Conscious thought is the steering wheel of manifestation. Use it with awareness — because it can drive you toward your desires, or toward your fears.

COMMON PITFALLS

- Obsessing over a desire without clarity, turning it into worry instead of vision.
- Repeating old doubts alongside affirmations ("I want this… but it probably won't happen").
- Forgetting to visualize with emotion — making the thought flat instead of alive.

EXERCISE: GUIDED VISUALIZATION PRACTICE

Visualization is one of the most powerful ways to strengthen a conscious thought. By picturing your desire in rich detail, you signal both your brain and Spirit that this thought matters — and you begin to align your energy with it.

Daily Practice (10–15 minutes):

1. **Find a quiet space.** Sit or lie down comfortably, close your eyes, and take a few slow, deep breaths. Allow your body to relax.

2. **Choose your desire.** Pick one thought you'd like to nurture (a new job, a vacation, healing, a relationship, etc.).
3. **Create the scene.** Imagine yourself already experiencing your desire. What do you see, hear, smell, taste, or touch? Let your senses fill in the picture.
4. **Feel the emotion.** Ask yourself: *How would I feel if this were already real?* Step into the joy, relief, excitement, or peace as if it is happening now.
5. **Affirm it silently.** Repeat a simple statement that reinforces the vision. For example:
   o *"I am grateful for the opportunities flowing to me."*
   o *"I welcome abundance and joy into my life."*
6. **Return gently.** Take a few deep breaths, then open your eyes and carry the feeling with you into your day.

Journaling Prompt (after visualization):

- What did I see or feel most vividly today?
- Did any new details appear in my vision?
- How did this visualization shift my mood or energy?

Tip: Repetition is key. The more often you practice, the stronger the neural pathways become — and the clearer the signal Spirit receives.

WANT TO GO DEEPER?

If you'd like a guided experience of this step, I've created a companion video for you on my YouTube channel. In it, I walk you through the process of **STEP 2: Recognize-Conscious Thought** so you can practice it in real time.

You can watch it here:
https://youtu.be/k_-klpH44_A
And/or
https://youtu.be/BxlZoMfkxWQ

Chapter 3 – Execute: Preparation

Theme: Manifestation requires action in the physical world.

E – Execute (aligned action, practical and decisive)
Dreams need energy. Taking small, aligned steps — writing it down, speaking it, preparing for it — tells Spirit and your subconscious: *"I am serious."* Execution is the bridge from mind to matter.

A conscious thought may feel powerful, but on its own, it is still only energy in the mind. To move that thought closer to reality, you must begin to interact with it in the **physical world**. This is the stage of **experience** — also known as preparation, energy, or action.

Think of this step as the **bridge** between thought and reality. Without it, the desire remains an idea. With it, the desire begins to take shape.

Preparation doesn't always mean leaping into the full experience right away. Often, it starts small:

- Making a phone call.
- Writing down your idea.
- Gathering information.
- Sharing your intention with a trusted friend.
- Taking the first, smallest step in alignment with your desire.

Each action sends a signal, both to your own brain and to Spirit, that you are serious. You are no longer just imagining — you are engaging.

Spirit responds to energy in motion. When you take even the tiniest step toward your vision, you shift the vibration around you. Doors open, synchronicities appear, and opportunities begin to reveal themselves.

Key Insight: Manifestation is not passive. It is an active collaboration between thought, Spirit, and your own willingness to prepare the way. The moment you begin to act, the invisible starts to become visible.

THE BRAIN AND ACTION: DOPAMINE, MOTIVATION, AND REWARD SYSTEMS

When you move from thought into action, your brain begins to engage in a very different way. Taking physical steps toward your desire activates the brain's **motivation and reward systems**, giving you both energy and encouragement to continue.

- **Dopamine: The Motivation Messenger**
  Dopamine is often called the "feel-good" chemical, but it's more accurately the **motivation molecule**. Each time you take a step toward your goal — researching flights, writing down your vision, or talking about your idea — your brain releases a little surge of dopamine. This creates a sense of anticipation and satisfaction that encourages you to keep going.
- **The Reward Pathway**
  This dopamine release activates the brain's **mesolimbic pathway**, which links effort with reward. The more often you take action and feel the reward, the stronger this pathway becomes. This is why small, consistent

steps matter — they create a cycle of action → reward → motivation → more action.

- **Momentum and Confidence**
As your brain experiences these mini rewards, it builds momentum. Suddenly, what once felt impossible begins to feel natural. The act of preparing and taking small steps rewires your brain to believe, *"Yes, this is happening. I can do this."*

From a spiritual perspective, this stage is powerful because your actions prove your commitment. Spirit responds not only to your repeated thoughts but to the **energy you put into motion**. Each action — no matter how small — is like watering the seed of manifestation. The brain supplies motivation, while Spirit supplies alignment.

Key Insight: Thoughts light the spark, but actions fuel the fire. Your brain is wired to reward you for movement, and Spirit amplifies what you are willing to act upon.

WHY MANY PEOPLE STOP HERE

For many, the stage of preparation feels both exciting and terrifying. This is where the dream begins to demand movement in the physical world, and that can stir up resistance.

- **Fear**: Taking action means risk. What if it doesn't work? What if you fail? Fear of the unknown often stops people from moving forward, keeping desires trapped in the mind instead of being expressed in reality.
- **Procrastination**: Action requires effort, and it's easy to delay. The voice of procrastination says, *"I'll do it tomorrow,"* or *"I need more time, more money, more certainty."* Days turn into weeks, and the seed never gets watered.
- **Doubt**: This is perhaps the strongest barrier. Doubt whispers, *"Maybe it's not possible. Maybe I don't*

deserve it." Doubt sabotages momentum, pulling the
energy back into the unconscious mind where it began.

- **Money Concerns**
  Finances are one of the most common reasons people
  abandon preparation. A thought like *"I can't afford it"*
  can shut the process down before it begins. Yet, money
  is often just energy in another form — it flows when
  matched with intention, creativity, and trust. Spirit does
  not withhold abundance, but if you focus only on lack,
  you block opportunities for provision to appear.
- **The Opinions of Others**
  Equally powerful are the voices around you. Friends,
  family, or colleagues may project their fears onto your
  dream:
    o *"That's unrealistic."*
    o *"It's too expensive."*
    o *"What if it doesn't work out?"*

  While their concerns may come from love or caution,
  they can weaken your confidence if you allow them to
  drown out your own inner voice. Manifestation requires
  discernment — to know when to listen to wise counsel,
  and when to silence the doubters so your vision can
  breathe.

These blocks are normal, but they are not final. The key is
recognizing that resistance always rises just before growth.
Fear, procrastination, and doubt are signs that you are on the
edge of expansion. If you stop here, your desire remains a
vision. But if you push through with even one small action, you
shift the balance — your brain rewards you, and Spirit sees your
commitment.

Key Insight: Most manifestations never fail because the
universe says "no." They fail because people stop here —
caught between thought and action. Overcoming this stage is
what separates dreams that fade from dreams that take form.

Money and opinions are not ultimate barriers; they are tests. They ask you, *"How committed are you to this desire?"* When you choose to keep preparing — even with small, affordable steps, or in quiet alignment despite criticism — you strengthen both your will and your signal to Spirit.

EXAMPLES OF PREPARATION IN ACTION

Preparation doesn't have to mean taking a giant leap. More often, it begins with small, intentional steps that signal your commitment to Spirit and to yourself.

- **Buying Workout Shoes Before Starting Exercise**
  Even before you begin the workout routine, you purchase new shoes. That single action tells your brain and Spirit: *"I am serious about moving my body."* The shoes become a physical reminder that you are preparing the way.
- **Creating a Vision Board**
  Gathering images, words, and symbols that represent your desire is another powerful act of preparation. A vision board transforms a thought into something tangible and visible. Each time you look at it, you reinforce your intention, bringing the energy closer to manifestation.
- **Researching Options**
  Looking up travel destinations, checking prices, or comparing programs may seem simple, but it moves your dream out of the realm of fantasy and into possibility.
- **Sharing Your Desire**
  Telling a trusted friend or loved one, *"I'm planning to do this,"* shifts the energy. Speaking the intention aloud makes it real, and Spirit hears the vibration in your words.

These examples show that preparation doesn't need to be overwhelming. Every small step waters the seed of your desire, helping it grow stronger and clearer.

Step 3

EXECUTE
Action/Experience
(preparation)

Calling a friend, getting a bathing suit/towel, going to the beach.

Ten minutes later, the thought has grown strong enough to move you into action. You grab your phone, call your friend, and ask if she wants to go swimming. She agrees right away.

With excitement building, you finish your work, head home to collect your swimsuit and towel, and then pick up your friend.

Together, you drive toward the beach, the anticipation of cool water making every step feel lighter.

In this moment, you are no longer just *thinking* about swimming — you are preparing for it. Each action, no matter how small, moves the idea out of imagination and into reality. Spirit sees your movement and responds, aligning the energy around you so that what was once only a thought is now unfolding in the physical world.

SPIRITUAL PERSPECTIVE EXAMPLE – STEP 3: EXECUTE—PREPARATION

Preparation is the point where energy begins to flow beyond the mind. It is no longer just a thought you hold — it is something you give form through words, actions, and tangible effort.

You decide to visit a travel agent and gather brochures. You flip through the pictures of beaches and hotels, imagining yourself there. The next day, you talk it over again with your friends, excitement growing with every conversation. Eventually, you put down a deposit on the trip. Soon after, you start sharing the news with your co-workers and friends: *"I'm going to Mexico!"*

From a spiritual perspective, this is the moment when Spirit knows you are serious. Your energy has shifted from possibility into preparation. Spirit can see your actions, hear your words, feel your enthusiasm, and know that you are aligning yourself with the desire.

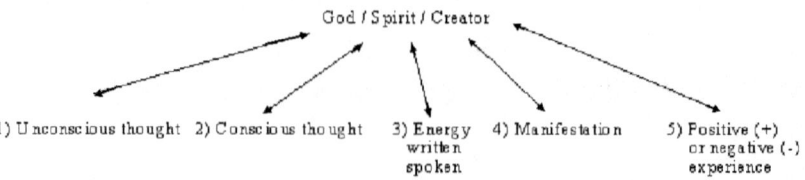

The seed of manifestation now has roots. Each small step in the physical world adds power to your intention in the spiritual world. Spirit responds to motion, and with each action, the invisible framework of your manifestation strengthens.

Key Insight: Spirit listens to thought, but Spirit responds to action. When you prepare with energy and intention, you declare to the universe: *"This is real. This is happening."*

TIP & WARNING: THE SHADOW SIDE OF PREPARATION

Preparation is where thoughts begin to take shape — where ideas gain momentum through action. But the same energy that builds can also block manifestation if misused.

The Shadow Side Looks Like:

- **Over-preparation:** Spending endless time planning, researching, or organizing without ever taking the leap. This creates the illusion of progress while avoiding real movement.
- **Scattered Action:** Jumping into too many things at once, diluting your energy so nothing gains traction.
- **Fear-Based Effort:** Acting out of desperation or panic rather than alignment, which often leads to missteps or burnout.
- **Listening Too Much to Others:** Allowing family, friends, or coworkers to talk you out of your steps before they even take root.

Tip: Choose *small, aligned actions* that feel both doable and meaningful. One clear step taken with conviction carries more power than a hundred scattered ones.

Warning: Preparation is not about perfection — it's about momentum. If you stay stuck in planning mode, you signal to

Spirit that you're not actually ready. Action, however small, tells Spirit: *"I mean this."*

Key Insight: Preparation is the bridge between thought and reality. Cross it with courage, not hesitation.

COMMON PITFALLS

- Getting stuck in overthinking without taking even small physical steps.
- Believing you need "perfect conditions" before acting.
- Letting fear, procrastination, or other people's opinions stop momentum.
- Taking frantic or scattered action instead of aligned, intentional steps.

EXERCISE: CREATE YOUR PREP PLAN

To move from thought into manifestation, you need to take grounded steps in the physical world. This exercise helps you design a simple "prep plan" to strengthen your desire and show Spirit that you are ready.

Step 1: Choose Your Desire
Pick one intention you want to manifest this month. (Example: starting a new wellness routine, planning a trip, launching a project, or inviting more abundance.)

Step 2: List 3 Physical Steps
Write down three small, tangible actions you can take this month to prepare. For example:

- If your desire is to **get healthier**, your steps might be:
    1. Buy a journal to track meals and moods.
    2. Stock your fridge with fresh, nourishing foods.
    3. Schedule one walk or workout with a friend.
- If your desire is to **travel**, your steps might be:

1. Research destinations and flight prices.
2. Set aside a small amount of money as a travel fund.
3. Request time off from work.

Step 3: Put Them on the Calendar
Assign a day and time for each action. Even small steps gain power when they are scheduled, not left floating in "someday."

Step 4: Reflection
At the end of the month, look back: Did you complete the steps? How did each one shift your energy or bring your desire closer?

Key Insight: Spirit notices motion. When you take even three small steps toward your vision, you are no longer wishing — you are preparing.

SMALL ALIGNED ACTIONS CREATE BIG MANIFESTATIONS

Manifestation doesn't always begin with giant leaps. More often, it begins with something small — a single, simple step that seems almost insignificant at the time.

- Buying a notebook becomes the first chapter of a new book.
- Saying "yes" to a coffee meeting leads to a life-changing partnership.
- Taking a five-minute walk opens the door to a long-term wellness routine.

When these actions are **aligned** — meaning they resonate with your intention and your deeper truth — they carry exponential power. Spirit recognizes the sincerity behind even the smallest steps, and the universe responds by arranging the next opportunity.

This is the snowball effect of manifestation: one step leads to another, and before long, momentum carries your desire forward more easily than you imagined.

Key Insight: Never underestimate the power of a small, aligned action. It may be the first domino in a series of events that transforms your entire reality.

WANT TO GO DEEPER?

If you'd like a guided experience of this step, I've created a companion video for you on my YouTube channel. In it, I walk you through the process of **STEP 3: Execute-Preparation** so you can practice it in real time.

You can watch it here:
https://youtu.be/-pBFvuC0cPc
And/or
https://youtu.be/8sQSeDpq4VA

Chapter 4 – Achieve: Manifestation

Theme: The desire materializes.

A – Achieve (Manifest: live it)

The desire materializes. You step into the experience of what you once only imagined. This is the moment where thought becomes reality — the fruit of alignment, action, and Spirit's partnership.

This is the moment you've been moving toward — the point where thought, energy, and preparation converge into lived reality. Manifestation is no longer something you are imagining or preparing for; it is something you are experiencing with your whole being.

You step fully into the reality you once only dreamed of. What began as an unconscious spark has passed through the stages of conscious thought and preparation, and now it has materialized in your life.

Manifestation is not abstract in this stage — it is tangible, undeniable, and physical. You can see it, touch it, taste it, and feel it. This is when you walk into the job you envisioned, embrace the partner you dreamed of, or stand on the beach you once only saw in your mind.

From a spiritual perspective, manifestation is Spirit's way of reflecting back to you what you have chosen, nurtured, and claimed. Spirit delivers what you aligned with — not by accident, but by design.

Key Insight: Manifestation is not the end of the journey, but the fulfillment of one cycle. You have brought the unseen into the seen, the imagined into the experienced.

THE BRAIN AND MANIFESTATION

When a desire becomes reality, your brain responds in powerful and measurable ways. This stage is about full immersion — your senses confirm what your mind once only imagined.

- **Sensory Integration**
  The brain lights up as you see, hear, touch, taste, and smell the experience. What was once a mental rehearsal in visualization is now anchored in your nervous system as a lived reality. The hippocampus stores it as memory, while the amygdala attaches emotion, strengthening its impact.
- **Dopamine and Reward**
  Manifestation triggers the release of dopamine, the brain's reward chemical. You feel joy, excitement, relief, or satisfaction because your brain recognizes: *"This is what I wanted, and now it is here."* This creates a reinforcing loop, motivating you to manifest again in the future.
- **The "This Is Real" Effect**
  Visualization primes the brain, but actual manifestation is even more powerful. The prefrontal cortex (decision-making center) and limbic system (emotional brain) integrate the experience. This "proof" solidifies your belief that manifestation works, strengthening the neural pathways that make future desires easier to imagine and achieve.

From a spiritual perspective, this is the moment of co-creation fulfilled: the brain celebrates with chemicals and pathways, while Spirit celebrates through synchronicities and alignment. The material and immaterial worlds meet here.

Key Insight: The brain rewards you for stepping into your manifested reality, creating both the memory and the motivation to continue the cycle of conscious creation.

SIGNS THAT MANIFESTATION HAS ARRIVED

Sometimes manifestation is obvious — you land the new job, you move into the new home, you arrive at the beach. Other times, it begins more subtly, showing up as signs that your desire is moving into form. These signals are Spirit's way of confirming that your alignment is working and that the reality you've called in is unfolding.

- **Synchronicities**
  You notice meaningful coincidences that seem too precise to be random. The right book appears, you meet someone who has exactly the information you need, or events line up in ways you couldn't have orchestrated yourself.
- **Invitations**
  Opportunities begin to present themselves. A friend offers to introduce you to someone in your field, a client calls unexpectedly, or you're asked to join something that aligns perfectly with your vision.
- **Opportunities**
  Doors that once felt closed suddenly open. Job postings, financial resources, or unexpected pathways appear, often with timing that feels divinely arranged.
- **Inner Confirmation**
  You feel a quiet sense of knowing — a calm assurance that what you asked for is on its way or already here.

This inner peace is just as much a sign as the external events.

These signs are Spirit's language of alignment. They remind you that manifestation isn't always a lightning strike; it's often a gentle unfolding, step by step, until one day you find yourself living inside the reality you once only imagined.

Key Insight: Manifestation rarely arrives out of nowhere. It announces itself through patterns, synchronicities, and invitations. When you notice these signs, you can step forward with trust, knowing your desire is being realized.

STORIES OF MANIFESTATIONS BIG AND SMALL

Manifestation doesn't always arrive as a life-changing event. Often, it shows up in small, everyday ways that remind you the process is always at work. Over time, these small manifestations build your trust so that larger desires can unfold.

- **The Parking Spot**
  You picture a space opening up near the entrance of a busy store. Moments later, a car pulls out, and you slide right in. Small as it may seem, this experience reinforces your ability to call things into reality.
- **The Phone Call**
  You've been thinking about a friend you haven't seen in years. Out of the blue, they call you that very evening. This is Spirit's way of showing that thought and energy ripple outward.
- **The Vacation**
  What started as a fleeting thought of Mexico turned into a detailed vision, then a plan, then tickets in your hand. Weeks later, you find yourself on the beach, swimming in the turquoise water you once only imagined.
- **The Dream Job**
  Someone visualizes working in a creative field. They

prepare by updating their portfolio and applying for positions. A month later, they receive an offer that matches not only the work they wanted but also the supportive environment they envisioned.

Big or small, each manifestation carries the same principle: a thought becomes focused, is nurtured with preparation, and finally blooms into experience. Spirit makes no distinction between summoning a parking space or creating a new career. The energy and alignment are the same — only the scale differs.

Key Insight: Pay attention to the small manifestations. They are Spirit's training ground, showing you that the process works so you can trust it with the bigger desires of your life.

STORY EXAMPLE –
STEP 4: ACHIEVE—MANIFESTATION

At last, the moment arrives. You and your friend reach the beach, drop your towels in the sand, and rush toward the water. The sun is still hot above you, but as soon as you dive beneath the surface, the heat melts away. Cool water surrounds you, refreshing every part of your body.

You laugh, splash, and swim with your friend — fully immersed in the experience you once only imagined. Just hours earlier, it was nothing more than a fleeting thought. Now, it is real, tangible, and undeniable.

This is manifestation: stepping into the reality that was once only a seed in your mind. Spirit has heard your intention and met your preparation with alignment. What you desired, you are now living.

SPIRITUAL PERSPECTIVE EXAMPLE – STEP 4: ACHIEVE—MANIFESTATION

Manifestation becomes complete when the desire you carried has fully materialized. It is no longer a thought, a plan, or an intention — it is a lived experience.

You step off the plane and land in Mexico, the very place that first flashed through your mind weeks ago. What began as a fleeting spark grew into a conscious thought, then into preparation, and now Spirit has aligned the path for you to arrive at your destination.

From a spiritual perspective, this is the essence of manifestation: Spirit provides exactly what you ask for and believe you deserve. There is no judgment, only response. This is why it is so important to be mindful of your desires — because Spirit does not filter "good" from "bad." Spirit reflects back the vibration and clarity you send.

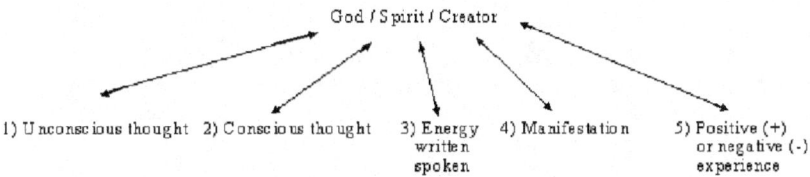

Key Insight: Always ask for what you desire to be aligned with your *highest good and best interest*. By adding this layer of intention, you invite Spirit to guide your manifestations toward outcomes that uplift, protect, and serve your soul's growth — not just your passing wishes.

TIP & WARNING: THE SHADOW SIDE OF MANIFESTATION

Manifestation is the moment when your desire becomes reality. It's joyful, empowering, and affirming — but this stage also has its shadows. Receiving what you asked for can create its own challenges if you're not prepared to handle it with awareness.

The Shadow Side Looks Like:

- **Attachment:** Clinging so tightly to what manifested that you fear losing it, blocking the flow of new blessings.
- **Entitlement:** Believing manifestation makes you superior or that Spirit "owes" you, which disconnects you from gratitude.
- **Dismissal:** Downplaying your manifestation as a coincidence, which weakens your trust in the process.
- **Escalation Trap:** Immediately chasing a bigger goal without pausing to reflect or appreciate the one already achieved.
- **Manifesting Without Alignment:** Sometimes what you manifested does arrive, but it doesn't feel good because it was born from ego, fear, or comparison rather than your higher good.

Tip: Pause to celebrate and anchor gratitude whenever a manifestation arrives — big or small. Gratitude stabilizes the energy and opens space for even more aligned experiences.

Warning: Spirit will mirror not only your desires but also your attitude toward them. If you receive without gratitude, you may block future flow. If you cling in fear, you may create the very loss you dread.

Key Insight: Manifestation is not the finish line — it's a sacred checkpoint. Treat each manifestation as both a gift and a teacher.

COMMON PITFALLS

- Missing the signs of arrival (synchronicities, opportunities, invitations).
- Downplaying or dismissing the manifestation once it happens ("Oh, that was just a coincidence").
- Forgetting gratitude which weakens the energy of the manifestation.
- Believing manifestation is the "end" instead of part of a larger cycle.

EXERCISE: WRITE YOUR MANIFESTATION MEMORY

One of the most powerful ways to strengthen your belief in manifestation is to look back at your own life and notice the times you've already done it. This exercise helps you recognize the process in action, building confidence that you can do it again and again.

Step 1: Recall a Manifestation
Think of a time when something you desired — big or small — became reality. It might have been finding the perfect home, meeting the right person, getting a job, or even something simple like finding a lost item or landing a parking spot.

Step 2: Break It Into Stages
Write down how that manifestation unfolded through each step of the DREAM Method:

1. **Unconscious Thought:** How did the first seed appear? (Ex: "I had a quick thought about wanting to move somewhere new.")

2. **Conscious Thought:** When did you start focusing on it more intentionally?
3. **Preparation:** What actions did you take that showed you were serious?
4. **Manifestation:** How did it finally appear in your reality?
5. **Reflection (+1):** Was it what you expected? How did the experience shape you?

Step 3: Reflect on the Pattern
As you write, notice how the process feels familiar. What did Spirit provide along the way? What signs or synchronicities appeared?

Step 4: Anchor the Lesson
Close your journal entry with one statement of gratitude: *"I see now that I manifested this, and I trust my ability to manifest again."*

Key Insight: Looking back at your own manifestations reminds you that this is not new or foreign — it's a process you've already lived. Awareness simply makes it repeatable.

WANT TO GO DEEPER?
If you'd like a guided experience of this step, I've created a companion video for you on my YouTube channel. In it, I walk you through the process of **STEP 4: Achieve-Manifestation** so you can practice it in real time.

You can watch it here:
https://youtu.be/8d918oADt2E
And/or
https://youtu.be/Szi-BLwnVak

Chapter 5 – Master: Reflection + or –

Theme: The hidden key that makes manifestation sustainable.

M – Master (Evolve: reflect, refine, and repeat)
Every manifestation brings wisdom. Mastery means reflecting on what worked, what didn't, and how it shaped you. With mastery, you evolve — ready to dream again, even bigger, even clearer.

Many people think manifestation ends when the desire is achieved. But the truth is, manifestation is not complete until you integrate the experience. This is why the fifth step — reflection — is so essential. It is the hidden key that makes manifestation sustainable and repeatable.

Reflection is the stage where you pause and ask: *What did this manifestation teach me? Did it fulfill my desire in the way I expected, or did it reveal something different?*

Without reflection, manifestation becomes a cycle of chasing one desire after another without understanding the deeper lessons. But with reflection, you gain the wisdom to decide whether to:

- **Repeat** the manifestation (if it brought joy and alignment).
- **Release** it (if it no longer serves you).
- **Refine** it (if it taught you something valuable, but needs adjustment for next time).

For example, someone may manifest a dream job only to realize the workload is unsustainable. Reflection helps them refine their next manifestation: not just any job, but one that balances purpose with peace. Another person may manifest a trip and find it so fulfilling that they want to repeat it annually.

Key Insight: Reflection turns manifestation from a one-time event into a conscious practice of growth. Spirit doesn't just deliver outcomes — Spirit also invites you to learn from them.

THE BRAIN AND REFLECTION: MEMORY, LEARNING, AND EMOTIONAL INTEGRATION

Reflection is not just a spiritual practice; it's also a neurological one. When you pause to reflect on your manifestation, your brain organizes the experience, creating patterns that guide your future choices.

- **Memory Consolidation**
  The hippocampus stores the details of the event, while the neocortex integrates them into long-term memory. Reflection strengthens these connections, making the experience easier to recall and learn from in the future.
- **Learning from Reward and Error**
  The brain's reward system evaluates outcomes: *Was this satisfying? Did it meet my expectations?* When you reflect, the prefrontal cortex (responsible for reasoning) compares the result with your original intention. If the experience was rewarding, the brain reinforces the pathway. If not, it flags the mismatch, encouraging refinement next time.
- **Emotional Integration**
  The amygdala attaches emotional meaning to the manifestation. Reflection allows you to consciously process these emotions, reducing lingering negativity or amplifying gratitude. This integration helps you carry

forward the feelings you want to repeat, while releasing those you do not.

- **Shaping Future Manifestations**
  Each time you reflect, you are essentially "reprogramming" your brain. You highlight what worked, learn from what didn't, and reset your inner compass. This makes your next manifestation more aligned, efficient, and sustainable.

From a spiritual perspective, this process mirrors the dialogue between you and Spirit. Your brain records the lessons; Spirit listens to how you interpret them. Together, they shape the blueprint for what you will call into your life next.

Key Insight: Reflection is the brain's way of closing the loop — and Spirit's way of preparing you for the next cycle of creation.

THE LOOP: MANIFESTATION → REFLECTION → NEW UNCONSCIOUS SEEDS

Reflection is not the end of the manifestation process — it is the reset button that begins the cycle all over again. Every manifestation you live through plants new seeds in your unconscious mind, whether you realize it or not.

Here's how the loop works:

1. **Manifestation:** You experience the reality you once desired.
2. **Reflection:** You pause to evaluate it. Was it joyful, disappointing, or surprising? What did you learn?
3. **New Unconscious Seeds:** Your reflection gives rise to fresh unconscious thoughts. If the experience was positive, you may unconsciously begin dreaming of repeating it or expanding it. If it was negative, you may

unconsciously form protective thoughts to avoid a similar outcome.

For example:

- You manifest a trip to Mexico. During reflection, you realize it was the best week of your year. That joy plants a new seed: *"I'd like to travel more often."*
- Or, you reflect and realize that while the beach was beautiful, you missed home. This too plants a seed: *"I'd rather manifest shorter trips closer to home."*

Spirit listens to the new seeds created in this reflective stage. Just as the first unconscious thought began the original cycle, your reflections shape the desires of tomorrow.

Key Insight: Manifestation is not linear — it is a living loop. Each experience feeds the next, and reflection is the hinge that turns endings into new beginnings.

EXAMPLES OF REFLECTION IN ACTION

Reflection is not only about celebrating what went well — it's also about learning from what did not. Every manifestation, even the ones that feel "unsuccessful," carries valuable insight that shapes your future desires.

- **The Job That Didn't Fit**
  You manifested a new position and were excited at first. But once you settled in, the environment felt toxic, and the workload was draining. Through reflection, you realize the job gave you clarity: not just *any* job will do — you want meaningful work in a supportive culture. Next time, your conscious thought will include *how* you want to feel in your career, not just the role itself.
- **The Relationship That Turned Sour**
  You attracted a partner who seemed perfect in the

beginning. Over time, though, patterns of control, dishonesty, or neglect appeared. Reflection helps you see that while you manifested companionship, you hadn't been clear about the qualities of love and respect you truly needed. This experience plants a new seed: the desire for a relationship rooted in trust and mutual growth.

- **The Financial Windfall That Vanished**
  Perhaps you manifested a sudden bonus, inheritance, or windfall. But without clarity or preparation, the money slipped away quickly. Reflection shows you that abundance requires not only receiving but also managing wisely. Spirit used the experience to teach stewardship.

Each of these examples shows that "unsuccessful" manifestations are never failures. They are teachers. Through reflection, you refine your desires and send clearer signals to Spirit for what you truly want moving forward.

Key Insight: Every manifestation offers a gift. The ones that disappoint often carry the richest lessons — shaping new seeds that align more closely with your highest good.

STORY EXAMPLE –
STEP 5: MASTER—REFLECTION

After an afternoon of swimming, you and your friend dry off, laugh about the fun you had, and drive back together. The sun is lower in the sky now, the heat is less intense, and you feel refreshed. Soon, you drop your friend off at her house and continue home.

As you drive, you reflect on the day. The simple thought of swimming that first appeared in your mind has now unfolded into a real experience. You notice how good it felt to cool off, to share the moment with a friend, and to enjoy the break from your usual routine.

In this quiet moment, you also recognize the power of reflection. Was the experience everything you hoped? Would you want to do it again? Did it bring you joy, or did it reveal something you might do differently next time?

This step determines whether the cycle repeats, shifts, or ends. Your positive reflection becomes the seed for future desires — perhaps to swim again, to plan more outings with friends, or to spend more time outdoors. Spirit hears this, too, and prepares to support the next cycle of manifestation.

SPIRITUAL PERSPECTIVE EXAMPLE – STEP 5: MASTER—REFLECTION

Reflection is the most important part of the manifestation cycle because it determines whether your desire continues, evolves, or dissolves. The outcome of your experience — positive or negative — sets the stage for what comes next.

For some, a manifestation is a **one-time wish**. For example, someone may dream of a vacation in Mexico, enjoy a week or two there, and then feel satisfied. The wish has been fulfilled, and there is no need to repeat it.

For others, the desire is ongoing. They don't just want to visit Mexico once; they want to live there permanently. Reflection helps them decide if the wish is something to hold onto, expand, or deepen.

And then there are those who discover that what they manifested was not what they truly wanted. Perhaps they move to Mexico, only to find that the fantasy fades and the reality is less fulfilling than they imagined. Reflection here is vital because it allows them to release the manifestation without judgment and create space for something more aligned.

From a spiritual perspective, Spirit always provides what you ask for and believe you deserve — whether positive or negative. Spirit does not choose for you; Spirit responds to your energy, thought patterns, and intentions.

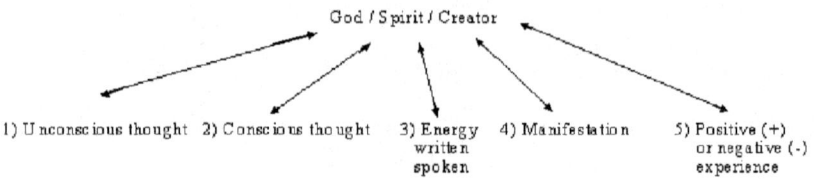

God / Spirit / Creator

1) Unconscious thought 2) Conscious thought 3) Energy written spoken 4) Manifestation 5) Positive (+) or negative (-) experience

- **If emotional issues or negative thoughts surround the manifestation**, they will sabotage the process, preventing it from lasting or repeating.
- **If your thought patterns remain genuine, grateful, and positive**, the manifestation can continue as long as you choose.
- **If you are not receiving what you want,** it is a sign to seek healing, guidance, or support to clear the blocks standing in your way.

Key Insight: Reflection teaches you that manifestation is not just about *getting what you want* but about *understanding what you've asked for.* Spirit always responds, but it is your reflection that decides whether the cycle repeats, refines, or ends.

SPIRITUAL INSIGHT

Reflection is more than looking back on what happened — it is the process of transforming your manifestation into wisdom. Every desire you bring to life carries a lesson. Some teach you joy, others reveal limits or illusions, but all of them guide you deeper into alignment with your true self.

When you pause to reflect, you give Spirit the opportunity to show you not only what you received, but *why* it came into your life and what it means for your soul's journey. Reflection turns experiences into teachers and outcomes into stepping stones.

This is why the +1 step is essential. Without reflection, manifestation can become a cycle of chasing — achieving one desire after another without deeper fulfillment. With reflection, manifestation becomes a cycle of awakening — each desire moving you closer to who you really are and what your spirit longs to express.

Key Insight: Reflection transforms manifestation into wisdom, aligning you more deeply with your true self. It ensures that manifestation is not just about *getting what you want* but about *becoming who you are meant to be.*

TIP & WARNING: THE SHADOW SIDE OF REFLECTION

Reflection is where wisdom is born — the stage that turns experiences into teachers and prepares you for the next cycle of manifestation. But when approached without awareness, reflection can become distorted, keeping you trapped instead of moving you forward.

The Shadow Side Looks Like:

- **Regret Loops:** Constantly replaying "what went wrong" without learning the lesson, which keeps you stuck in disappointment.
- **Self-Blame:** Turning reflection into self-criticism — *"I should have known better"* — rather than compassionate growth.

- **Denial:** Refusing to look at uncomfortable truths, which prevents healing and repeats old patterns.
- **Clinging:** Holding onto a manifestation long after it has served its purpose, blocking new seeds from being planted.
- **Comparison:** Using reflection to measure yourself against others instead of focusing on your own journey.

Tip: Approach reflection with curiosity, not judgment. Ask: *"What did this experience teach me? What do I want to carry forward, and what do I want to release?"*

Warning: Reflection without compassion becomes rumination. Spirit is not punishing you — Spirit is guiding you. If you reflect harshly, you may reinforce limiting beliefs rather than transform them.

Key Insight: Reflection is the reset key. Done with awareness and self-love, it ensures that manifestation evolves into wisdom instead of cycles of regret.

COMMON PITFALLS

- Skipping reflection altogether and rushing into the next desire.
- Clinging to a manifestation that no longer serves you.
- Interpreting an "unsuccessful" manifestation as failure instead of feedback.
- Ignoring the wisdom that obstacles reveal.

EXERCISE: CREATE A REFLECTION JOURNAL

Reflection becomes more powerful when you make it a conscious practice. By writing down your experiences, you train both your brain and Spirit to recognize patterns, refine your desires, and strengthen future manifestations.

Step 1: Set Up Your Journal
Take a notebook or open a digital document. Draw a line down the center of each page to create two columns:

- Left column: **What Worked**
- Right column: **What Didn't**

Step 2: After Each Manifestation
When you experience a manifestation — big or small — pause to reflect and fill in both columns.

Example:

- *Manifestation:* Trip to Mexico
    - **What Worked:** Felt joy, deep rest, meaningful connection with friends.
    - **What Didn't:** Overspent money, sunburn, missed my family at home.

Step 3: Look for Patterns
After a few entries, review your notes. Do the same challenges keep appearing? Do certain actions or mindsets always lead to better results? These patterns show you where to repeat, release, or refine.

Step 4: Close With Gratitude
No matter what you write, always end with a statement of thanks: *"I am grateful for this experience and the lessons it taught me."* Gratitude transforms reflection from criticism into wisdom.

Key Insight: Your Reflection Journal becomes a mirror of your growth. Over time, it will show you that manifestation isn't luck — it's a process you are mastering with clarity and awareness.

WANT TO GO DEEPER?

If you'd like a guided experience of this step, I've created a companion video for you on my YouTube channel. In it, I walk you through the process of **STEP 5: Master-Reflection** so you can practice it in real time.

You can watch it here:
https://youtu.be/l-9L4682_zg
and/or
https://youtu.be/EJhqhzZZIXQ

Chapter 6 – At Any Point, Manifestation Can Be Stopped

Theme: Awareness = choice.

Manifestation is often spoken of as if it were automatic — as though once a thought is planted, it must unfold into reality. But the truth is, the process is not fixed. It is flexible. You always have the power of choice.

Returning to the diagram, notice how each step flows into the next: unconscious thought, conscious thought, preparation, manifestation, and reflection. Yet at every stage, there is an opening — an opportunity to pause, redirect, or stop the process altogether.

- A fleeting unconscious thought can be dismissed before it takes root.
- A conscious thought can be released if you realize it doesn't serve you.
- Preparation can be halted if you sense the timing isn't right.
- Even after manifestation, reflection can show you it's time to let go or move in a new direction.

This flexibility is empowering. It means you are not at the mercy of every thought or desire that arises. You are the gardener of your own mind. Some seeds you nurture, others you pull up before they grow.

Spirit honors this freedom. Spirit responds to the thoughts and actions you choose to sustain, not to every impulse that passes through. Awareness gives you the ability to decide: *Do I want this? Does this align with my highest good? Am I ready to release it and create something new?*

Key Insight: Manifestation is not a one-way street. Awareness allows you to stop, redirect, or refine at any point. In this way, you are never trapped by your thoughts — you are always free to choose.

WHEN MANIFESTATIONS STALL

Even with the DREAM Method, there will be times when your manifestations feel slow, stuck, or incomplete. This does not mean the process isn't working — it means there is something to notice, refine, or realign.

Why Manifestations Stall

1. **Timing** – Spirit often operates on a larger rhythm than our human impatience. Some manifestations require conditions, people, or opportunities to align first. Think of it like planting a seed: you cannot rush the sprout before the season is ready.
2. **Clarity** – Vague desires create vague results. If you "kind of" want something, the universe "kind of" delivers. Lack of focus scatters your energy.
3. **Subconscious Conflict** – Old beliefs, fears, or emotional wounds may silently block your desire. You might say, *"I want wealth,"* but deep down believe, *"I don't deserve it."* That conflict stalls the cycle.

How to Reset Without Frustration

1. **Pause and Reflect**
   - Ask: *Where am I in the DREAM cycle?*
   - Am I drifting without recognizing? Recognizing without executing? Or am I stuck in reflection, never planting again?
2. **Clear the Conflict**
   - If resistance shows up (fear, doubt, guilt), name it. Journaling, energy healing, therapy, or prayer can help clear the block so your energy flows freely again.
3. **Refocus the Intention**
   - Rewrite your desire in clear, affirmative language. Instead of *"I don't want debt,"* say *"I welcome financial freedom."*
4. **Take One Aligned Action**
   - Even a small, simple step tells Spirit you are back in motion. Look up a resource, make a phone call, shift your environment. Action resets energy.
5. **Surrender Timing**
   - Affirm: *"This or something better, in perfect timing, for my highest good."* This releases pressure and restores trust.

Remember: a stalled manifestation isn't failure — it's feedback. It shows you where more clarity, patience, or inner alignment is needed. With each reset, you strengthen your ability to live the DREAM with grace and persistence.

Emergency Reset: 2–3 Minute Practice

Close your eyes. Take one deep, steady breath in… and let it go.
Say silently: **"Pause. Reset. Redirect."**

1. **Drift** — Notice what thought just floated in. Is it fear, doubt, or procrastination? Name it. *"This is fear." "This is resistance."*
2. **Recognize** — Choose one thought that supports you instead. *"I am capable." "This step matters." "Spirit walks with me."*
3. **Execute** — Decide on one small, doable action you can take in the next 5 minutes. (Write one sentence, send one message, take one breath.)
4. **Achieve** — Imagine how it will feel once it's done. See yourself relieved, smiling, proud.
5. **Master** — Whisper: **"Every block is feedback. I am stronger, clearer, and back on track."**

Take one more breath. Open your eyes. Do the next small step now.

This works as a **"pocket practice"** readers can memorize and use anywhere—before a meeting, while procrastinating at their desk, or when fear spikes.

STORY EXAMPLE – STEP 1-5
Examples: How Manifestation Can Be Stopped at Any Stage

Manifestation is not a rigid chain of events — it is a living process, and life always offers you opportunities to pause, redirect, or stop altogether. Here are some scenarios that show how the cycle can shift at different stages:

1. **Unconscious or Conscious Stage**
   A co-worker suddenly hurts himself and you must take him to the hospital. The thought of swimming is forgotten, replaced by a more urgent responsibility. The seed never grows.

2. **Unconscious Seed Dissolves Naturally**
   It begins to rain. The cool air relieves the heat, and the thought of swimming is no longer appealing. Spirit notes the shift, and the desire dissolves.

3. **Preparation Redirected**
   Your friend tells you about another invitation — a party that sounds more fun. Instead of packing your swimsuit, you prepare for the party instead. The original manifestation cycle ends, and a new one begins.

4. **Manifestation Blocked by Circumstances**
   On the way to the beach, your car breaks down, or the road is blocked. You never arrive at the water. The process is interrupted, showing how external conditions can shift manifestation outcomes.

5. **Reflection Changes the Cycle**
   You do make it to the beach, but your friend has never swum before, and both of you nearly drown. For her, it becomes a traumatic experience — she vows never to swim again. For you, however, it is a minor setback. You chalk it up to bad luck and continue to enjoy swimming in the future. Reflection decides whether the cycle continues or ends.

Key Insight: These examples show that manifestation is never "set in stone." At any point, life events, external influences, or your own choices can alter the process. What matters is your awareness — recognizing when to release, when to redirect, and when to try again.

WANT TO GO DEEPER?

If you'd like a guided experience of this step, I've created a companion video for you on my YouTube channel. In it, I walk you through two **Scenarios** so you can understand it in real time.

You can watch it here:
https://youtu.be/rgg5neoxN2Y
and/or
https://youtu.be/BdIO0XZUJDg

WHY SOME MANIFESTATIONS ARE EASIER THAN OTHERS

Not all manifestations require the same amount of alignment, preparation, or cooperation. Some desires are simple, common, and widely available, while others are rare, complex, or involve many people and resources.

Take something as basic as a **pen or pencil**. If you suddenly need one, chances are you'll find one within minutes — on your desk, in a drawer, at a store, or even in the garbage. Pens are everywhere, inexpensive, and easy to access. The thought is small, the action is minimal, and the manifestation arrives quickly.

Now compare that with something like a **trip to the moon**. The desire may be just as strong, but the manifestation involves billions of dollars, advanced technology, government approval, trained astronauts, and global cooperation. It is not impossible — humanity has done it — but it requires massive alignment, preparation, and resources.

This contrast shows that manifestation operates on the same principles no matter what you desire, but the **scale of effort and alignment** differ.

- **Simple manifestations** often appear quickly because they are already abundant and require little preparation.
- **Complex manifestations** may take months, years, or even decades, because Spirit must align many moving pieces and people to bring them into reality.

Key Insight: Whether it's a pen or a trip to the moon, the process is the same. The difference lies in scale. Spirit responds equally, but the universe must organize the manifestation according to what's needed for it to come into form.

WHEN OTHERS INFLUENCE YOUR MANIFESTATIONS

Manifestation is deeply personal, but it doesn't exist in isolation. Family, friends, coworkers, teachers, and authority figures can all affect how you see yourself and what you believe is possible. Sometimes their influence supports your vision — other times, it blocks or sabotages it.

- **The Weight of Opinions**
  A parent may tell you that your dream is unrealistic. A friend may laugh at your idea. A boss may discourage you from leaving for a new opportunity. Words carry energy, and if you absorb them, their doubt can plant seeds of fear in your unconscious mind.
- **Emotional Pressure**
  Sometimes, people unintentionally make you feel guilty for wanting more. *"Why would you move away when your family is here?"* or *"Who do you think you are to go after that?"* Emotional manipulation can keep you stuck in old patterns rather than moving forward into your true desires.
- **Authority Conditioning**
  Teachers, bosses, or mentors often shape our beliefs about what we're capable of. Praise can fuel confidence, but criticism can echo for years. If you've ever stopped

short of a dream because *"someone told me I couldn't,"* you've experienced this influence.

- **Energy of Envy or Fear**
  Not everyone celebrates when you grow. Some people project envy, fear, or resentment, sending energy that can interfere with your momentum if you aren't grounded in your own clarity.

How to Protect Your Manifestation:

1. **Discern the Source:** Ask yourself, *"Is this my truth or their fear?"*
2. **Set Energetic Boundaries:** Visualize a shield of light around you that allows love in but deflects doubt or negativity.
3. **Affirm Your Choice:** Speak your desire with conviction: *"This is aligned with my highest good."*
4. **Seek Supportive Voices:** Surround yourself with people who encourage your growth, not those who diminish it.

Key Insight: Others may try to shape your reality with their words or actions, but Spirit responds to *your vibration, not theirs*. When you stand in awareness and alignment, no outside opinion can block what you are truly committed to manifesting.

WHEN MORE THAN ONE PERSON IS INVOLVED IN A MANIFESTATION

Some manifestations are simple — you decide, you prepare, and you receive. But others, especially bigger desires, involve many people, each bringing their own intentions and energy into the process.

Take the example of purchasing a home. This single manifestation involves:

- **You** – holding the vision of the house you want.

- **Your Immediate Family** – agreeing on size, location, or price.
- **The Banker or Mortgage Lender** – deciding whether to approve the loan.
- **The Seller** – choosing to accept or reject your offer.
- **The Buyer of Your Current Home** (if applicable) – whose decision may impact your ability to move forward.
- **Lawyers, Inspectors, Realtors** – whose actions and timelines can affect the process.

When multiple people are involved, the manifestation becomes a **network of intentions.** Each person's choices and alignment can influence how quickly, smoothly, or successfully the outcome materializes.

How to Navigate Shared Manifestations:

1. **Stay Centered in Your Vision**
   Even when others are involved, keep your own focus clear. Your vibration anchors the process.
2. **Allow Flexibility**
   Sometimes Spirit has to rearrange the puzzle pieces. If a seller backs out or financing shifts, trust that the delay may lead to an even better outcome.
3. **Acknowledge Others' Free Will**
   You cannot control the desires or actions of others. Instead of resisting, affirm: *"If not this, then something better, aligned with my highest good."*
4. **Collaborate with Spirit**
   Pray, meditate, or set an intention not just for yourself, but for all involved. For example: *"May everyone in this process receive the outcome that serves their highest good."*

Key Insight: When more than one person is involved, manifestation becomes a co-creation on a larger scale. Spirit orchestrates the moving parts, aligning not just your good, but the good of everyone connected to the outcome.

MANIFESTATION BLOCK → FIX CHART

Block	Fix / Reframe
Lack of clarity (not sure what you really want)	Rewrite the goal in simple, specific, positive terms. Ask: *What do I want instead?*
Conflicting desires (wanting two opposing things)	Prioritize. Choose the desire that feels most aligned right now; save the other for later.
Doubt in yourself	Affirm: *"I am capable and learning. Every small step proves progress."* Keep a "Win Log" of past successes.
Doubt in Spirit / the process	Add the Highest Good clause: *"This or something better, in perfect timing."* Look back at a time something aligned unexpectedly.
Fear of failure	Reframe: Failure = feedback, not final. Ask: *What can this teach me?* Take one safe "trial step."
Fear of success	Journal: *What changes if I succeed?* Create safety by setting healthy boundaries and pacing growth.
Fear of judgment	Affirm: *"Others' opinions are theirs, not my truth."* Surround

Block	Fix / Reframe
	yourself with supportive voices.
Fear of responsibility/change	Break the goal into micro-steps. Let yourself "test-drive" success before fully committing.
Negative self-talk	Cancel–Reset–Redirect: Notice it, stop it, replace it with a supportive truth.
Limiting beliefs (from past/childhood)	Write the old belief → Replace with new belief. Example: *"Money is scarce"* → *"Money flows to me in many ways."*
Unhealed trauma/emotional wounds	Seek healing: therapy, EFT, Reiki, journaling. Acknowledge: *"This block is a teacher."*
Guilt about wanting more	Affirm: *"My joy uplifts others. Abundance is not selfish — it ripples outward."*
Feeling unworthy	Daily mirror affirmation: *"I am worthy of love, success, and joy."* List 5 qualities you already bring to the world.
Lack of time/energy	Timebox 10–15 minutes. Eliminate or delegate one low-value task. Refill energy first (rest, nutrition, grounding).

Block	Fix / Reframe
Lack of money/resources	Reduce goal to a starter version. Ask: *What can I do with what I already have?* Explore alternative options (borrow, trade, free).
Lack of skills/knowledge	Identify one skill gap → Commit to one learning step (book, mentor, tutorial) this week.
Procrastination	Break task into a 5-minute action. Start tiny. Use a timer. Progress, not perfection.
Perfectionism	Reframe: Done is better than perfect. Progress creates clarity.
Impatience	Affirm: *"I trust divine timing."* Celebrate micro-progress daily.
Past disappointments	Release with reflection: What did I learn? How does that protect/prepare me now?
Overthinking/over-analyzing	Choose one action and commit to testing it. Action creates clarity.
Dependence on others' approval	Affirm: *"My worth is not defined by others' opinions."* Practice making one small decision daily without seeking validation.

Block	Fix / Reframe
Toxic relationships/environment	Create boundaries. Add one supportive influence (friend, group, mentor).
Carrying responsibility for others' happiness	Reframe: *"I am responsible for my growth; others are responsible for theirs."*
Not trusting intuition	Daily practice: Write "first thought" in situations. Strength grows with use.
Attachment to old stories/identity	Ask: *"Who am I becoming?"* Write a new "I am" identity statement.
Forgetting action	Use the DREAM daily log. Put one Execute step on your calendar every day.
Refusing to release what no longer serves you	Practice letting go: donate, release, forgive. Affirm: *"By clearing space, I welcome better."*

The Power of Belief in Manifestation

Belief is one of the most powerful forces in manifestation. A single person's belief can influence their own reality, but when many people share the same belief, it can shape the collective world we live in.

Think of something simple, like a **pencil**. Because nearly everyone believes in the usefulness of pencils, they are produced in massive numbers and made readily available. Your manifestation of a pencil is almost instantaneous — the belief of millions ensures that pencils are everywhere, from schools and offices to shops and even garbage bins.

Now compare that with something extraordinary, like a **trip to the moon**. For centuries, such an idea would have been dismissed as fantasy. But once enough people began to believe it was possible — scientists, governments, inventors, dreamers — resources, time, and energy aligned. Collective belief fueled decades of research and preparation until, in 1969, the first humans walked on the moon. What was once unthinkable became reality through the power of shared belief.

This also explains why **time matters in manifestation**. Small, everyday manifestations can be nearly instant because they align with widespread belief and availability. Larger, less common manifestations may take years or generations, because collective belief must shift to make them possible.

History gives us countless examples:

- For centuries, people believed the **Earth was flat** and that sailing too far would lead to falling off the edge. It wasn't until bold explorers tested the belief, and evidence replaced fear, that the collective shifted to a new reality.

- Airplanes, electricity, and the internet all began as ideas many thought impossible. Over time, collective belief grew strong enough to call them into form.

Key Insight: The speed and scale of manifestation often depend on belief. The stronger your personal belief, the faster your desires align. And when collective belief gathers around an idea, it has the power to reshape what humanity sees as possible.

THE MINDSET OF MANIFESTATION: DEMAND AND COMMAND

One of the most overlooked aspects of manifestation is **mindset**. Many people approach their desires with hesitation: *"I hope this works... maybe if I'm lucky... I'll try."* But manifestation is not activated by wishy-washy thinking. It responds to clarity, conviction, and authority.

Jesus demonstrated this principle in its highest form. He did not beg or plead for miracles. He did not "hope" water would turn into wine, or that the sick would be healed. He **demanded and commanded** with certainty: *"Rise and walk." "Lazarus, come forth."* His words carried the authority of belief so complete that doubt had no place in them.

It was this mindset — this unwavering demonstration of manifestation — that drew crowds and followers. People recognized that he was not only teaching about Spirit but embodying Spirit's power. His clarity and authority challenged the systems of control in his time.

And so, the very abilities that revealed his divine alignment also made him a threat. The religious leaders and political authorities feared what would happen if people continued to believe and follow him. The crucifixion was not just about punishment — it was about silencing the power of one who had proven that manifestation, faith, and authority could overturn the old order.

Key Insight: Manifestation requires conviction. When you demand and command with clarity — not from ego, but from alignment with Spirit and the highest good — the universe responds. Doubt scatters energy; conviction concentrates it.

HOW TO INTERRUPT NEGATIVE MANIFESTATIONS

Just as you can nurture positive manifestations, you can also unintentionally feed negative ones. Fear, worry, and toxic thought cycles act like seeds, too — and if left unchecked, they can grow into realities you do not want. The good news is that awareness gives you the power to interrupt them at any stage.

Catch It Early

The most effective way to stop a negative manifestation is to interrupt it before it gains momentum. Negative thoughts often start small, slipping in unnoticed: a brief worry about money, a flash of fear about health, a moment of doubt about your worth. Left unchecked, these seeds can take root and grow.

The secret is **awareness.** The moment you notice the thought, call it by name.

- When a financial worry arises, say: *"This is fear about money."*
- When self-doubt sneaks in, say: *"This is insecurity speaking."*
- When you replay an old mistake, say: *"This is guilt."*

By labeling the thought, you separate **yourself** from it. You are no longer inside the fear — you are observing it. Neuroscience shows that naming emotions activates the prefrontal cortex (the reasoning part of your brain) and calms the amygdala (the fear center). Spiritually, this act of naming breaks the unconscious loop and pulls the thought into conscious awareness, where you can choose differently.

Think of it like catching a spark before it lights a fire. The earlier you notice, the easier it is to extinguish.

Once you've named it, you can:

- Take a deep breath and say, *"I release this thought."*
- Replace it with a positive statement: *"I am safe and supported."*
- Or redirect your focus: move your body, write it down and tear up the page, or pray for clarity.

Key Insight: Fear and worry lose their power the moment you shine light on them. Naming the thought is your first line of defense — it weakens the grip of negativity and reopens the door to conscious creation.

Shift the Energy

Even when you catch a negative thought early, sometimes its energy lingers — like an echo in your body and emotions. If left unattended, that echo can pull you back into the loop. The key is to shift the energy so your mind and Spirit reset into balance.

Think of it as changing the channel on a radio. If fear or worry is playing, you don't argue with it — you tune into a different frequency.

Here are some powerful ways to shift the energy:

- **Deep Breathing**
  Take a slow inhale for a count of four, hold for four, exhale for four, and pause for four. This simple practice (sometimes called "box breathing") calms the nervous

system, reduces anxiety, and signals to your brain: *"I am safe."*

- **Prayer or Intention**
  Speak directly to Spirit: *"I release this fear and ask for guidance and peace."* Prayer isn't about begging — it's about aligning your energy with a higher source and remembering you are not alone in your manifestation journey.

- **Meditation or Stillness**
  Close your eyes and imagine light filling your body from head to toe. Visualize the negative thought dissolving like mist in the sun. Meditation shifts you from the mind's noise to Spirit's calm, where new clarity can emerge.

- **Movement**
  Energy loves motion. A brisk walk, dancing to a favorite song, or even shaking out your arms and legs can break stagnant loops. Movement tells your body it doesn't have to stay stuck in fear — it can literally move forward.

- **Grounding Practices**
  If your thoughts feel scattered, reconnect with the earth: step outside barefoot, touch a tree, or hold a grounding crystal like hematite or smoky quartz. Grounding roots your energy, reminding you that you are stable, supported, and connected.

Key Insight: Energy cannot be destroyed — but it can be transformed. By shifting fear into breath, prayer, meditation, or movement, you rewire your nervous system and redirect Spirit's attention toward balance and creation.

Reframe the Thought

Thoughts carry momentum. If you constantly tell yourself, *"I'm always unlucky,"* or *"Things never work out for me,"* your subconscious begins to accept these statements as truth. Spirit hears them as instructions, and your reality bends to match them.

The good news? A single reframe can interrupt that toxic cycle and redirect the flow of energy. By choosing a new thought, you plant a healthier seed that Spirit and your subconscious can nurture instead.

Here's how to reframe effectively:

1. **Notice the Old Belief**
   Pay attention to the words you use when you talk to yourself. Do you hear absolutes like *always, never, nothing, nobody*? These are signs of limiting beliefs.
2. **Flip It Into Possibility**
   Take the old thought and shift it into an opening.

- Old: *"I'm always unlucky."*
- New: *"I am open to new possibilities."*
- Old: *"This always goes wrong."*
- New: *"I trust that solutions are available."*
- Old: *"Nobody appreciates me."*
- New: *"I attract people who value and respect me."*

3. **Anchor It With Emotion**
   Say the new belief aloud, slowly, and feel it in your body. Place your hand on your heart, smile, or breathe deeply as you speak it. Emotion supercharges the reframe, turning words into energy.
4. **Repeat Until Natural**
   At first, the new thought may feel awkward or forced. That's normal — you're rewiring old pathways. With

repetition, the brain forms new connections (neurons that fire together, wire together), and soon the positive reframe feels just as natural as the old limiting thought once did.

Key Insight: Reframing doesn't deny reality — it reshapes your perspective. By planting new thoughts, you shift the vibration of your inner world, and Spirit responds by aligning your outer world to match.

Seek Support

Some negative manifestations are easy to interrupt on your own. A quick reframe or grounding practice can reset your energy. But sometimes the roots run deeper. Old trauma, long-held limiting beliefs, or unresolved emotional pain can keep resurfacing, sabotaging your efforts no matter how often you try to "think positive."

That's when seeking support becomes essential. You don't have to carry everything alone — and Spirit often works through other people to bring you the help you need.

Types of Support That Can Help:

- **Therapy or Counseling**
  Traditional therapy can uncover hidden wounds, patterns, or subconscious beliefs that drive self-sabotage. Talking it through in a safe space often loosens the hold of what you've carried for years.
- **Energy Healing**
  Practices like Reiki, BodyTalk, EFT (Emotional Freedom Technique), Touch for Health, or other energy modalities can clear blockages stored in the body and aura. These methods work with subtle energy systems to release what words alone cannot reach.

- **Coaching or Mentorship**
  Sometimes what you need most is encouragement and accountability. A coach or mentor helps you identify blind spots, hold steady to your goals, and rewire your mindset step by step.
- **Spiritual Guidance**
  Prayer, meditation circles, or working with a trusted spiritual teacher can reconnect you with faith and remind you that Spirit is always ready to help. Guidance often comes through wisdom, synchronicities, or messages you might not notice alone.

How to Know When You Need Support:

- You feel stuck in the same repeating cycles.
- Your refraining practices only last temporarily.
- Negative thoughts feel overwhelming or uncontrollable.
- You sense "something deeper" is holding you back.

Key Insight: Seeking support is not weakness — it is wisdom. Spirit provides many pathways for healing, and other people's gifts may be the bridge to help you clear what you cannot shift alone. The sooner you release the roots, the faster you return to alignment with conscious creation.

Add the Higher Good Clause

Not every desire you hold will serve your growth. Sometimes what you think you want is shaped by fear, ego, or momentary impulse. Spirit will answer regardless, but if the manifestation would ultimately harm you, it may feel more like sabotage than success.

This is why it's wise to add a safeguard to every affirmation, intention, or goal:

"May this be for my highest good and best interest."

This simple clause does three powerful things:

1. **It Aligns With Spirit's Wisdom**
   Spirit sees the bigger picture — including things you cannot yet understand. By adding the clause, you invite Spirit to adjust the details, ensuring that the outcome supports your soul's journey rather than distracting or damaging it.
2. **It Redirects Energy Away From Harm**
   If your desire would lead to negative consequences — like a toxic relationship, financial strain, or poor health — the higher good clause blocks or delays it. Instead, it reroutes the energy toward an outcome that nourishes rather than drains you.
3. **It Keeps You in Flow**
   Without this safeguard, you might spend years manifesting something only to discover it wasn't what you truly needed. With it, you stay in flow — even if one door closes, you can trust Spirit is guiding you to a better one.

Example:

- Without the clause: You may manifest a high-paying job that leaves you exhausted and unfulfilled.
- With the clause: You may manifest a different job that pays well *and* supports your health, joy, and growth.

Key Insight: Adding *"for my highest good and best interest"* is like handing Spirit the map and saying, *"Here's where I think I want to go, but guide me to the best destination."* It transforms manifestation from wish-fulfillment into soul-alignment.

PRACTICES TO SHIFT FROM UNCONSCIOUS SABOTAGE → CONSCIOUS CREATION

Unconscious sabotage happens when old patterns, limiting beliefs, or hidden fears shape your thoughts without your awareness. Left unchecked, these thoughts can steer manifestation in directions you don't actually want. The key is to bring them into the light — to transform them into conscious, intentional creation.

Here are some practices to help with that shift:

Awareness Journaling

One of the simplest yet most powerful tools for transforming unconscious sabotage into conscious creation is **awareness journaling**. Most people have 60,000–70,000 thoughts a day, and the majority of them repeat without notice. By capturing even a few of these thoughts in writing, you begin to see patterns that were invisible before.

How to Practice Awareness Journaling:

1. **Set Aside Five Minutes Each Evening**
   This doesn't need to be long or complicated. Keep a notebook by your bed or use a digital notes app. The point is consistency, not length.
2. **Write Down Key Thoughts From the Day**
   Don't try to capture everything. Just recall the thoughts that stood out — the ones that had emotion behind them. Examples:
   o *"I'll never get ahead at work."*
   o *"I really enjoyed talking to that new friend."*
   o *"I'm too tired to exercise."*
   o *"I'm proud of myself for finishing that project."*
3. **Look for Recurring Themes**
   After a few days, notice what repeats. Are the themes

supportive ("I can do this," "Things always work out for me"), or sabotaging ("I'm unlucky," "I'll never change")? Repetition reveals where your energy is flowing — and what you're unconsciously manifesting.

4. **Label Each Thought**
Beside each entry, mark it as **Supportive** or **Sabotaging.** This simple step moves the thought from unconscious to conscious. It tells your brain: *"I see this. I can choose differently."*

5. **Reframe the Sabotaging Thoughts**
Take one sabotaging thought and rewrite it into a supportive affirmation. For example:
   o Sabotage: *"I'll never get ahead at work."*
   o Reframe: *"I am open to new opportunities that advance my career."*

6. **Close With Gratitude**
End each journaling session by writing down one thing you're grateful for. Gratitude shifts your energy and sets your subconscious on a positive track before sleep.

Why It Works:

- Psychologically: Writing slows the mind down, making unconscious thoughts visible.
- Neurologically: Naming and reframing thoughts activates the prefrontal cortex, reducing the emotional charge of fear or doubt.
- Spiritually: Awareness transforms scattered energy into focused intention. Spirit can only respond clearly when you are clear.

Key Insight: Awareness journaling is like shining a flashlight into the corners of your mind. What was once hidden can no longer control you. By noticing, labeling, and reframing, you reclaim your power to create.

Pattern Interrupts

Negative loops — cycles of worry, self-criticism, or doubt — often repeat without resistance because they feel familiar. The longer they run, the stronger the neural pathway becomes, and the more natural the sabotage feels. A **pattern interrupt** is a deliberate action that breaks the cycle in the moment and creates space for a new thought to take root.

How to Use a Pattern Interrupt:

1. **Notice the Loop**
   Awareness is the first step. Do you find yourself rehearsing the same worry about money? Criticizing yourself for a mistake? Doubting whether you're worthy of success? That's a loop.
2. **Stop It Immediately**
   Say out loud (or firmly in your mind):
   "Cancel. Reset. Redirect."

- *Cancel* = This thought does not serve me.
- *Reset* = I choose to clear the slate.
- *Redirect* = I turn my energy toward what I do want.

Speaking it aloud engages your nervous system more powerfully than thinking it silently — it jolts you out of autopilot.

3. **Replace With a Supportive Thought**
   Immediately follow the interruption with a new statement aligned with your intention. Example:

- Loop: *"I'm never going to have enough money."*
- Interrupt: *"Cancel. Reset. Redirect."*
- Reframe: *"I am open to receiving financial abundance in surprising ways."*

4. **Anchor the Shift Physically**
   Add a small action to reinforce the new thought. Take a deep breath, tap your chest, clap your hands, or stand tall with your shoulders back. This signals your body that the old energy is gone and a new pattern is beginning.
5. **Repeat Until Automatic**
   The first few times, it may feel forced. But with repetition, the brain learns: negative loop → interruption → supportive thought. Over time, this becomes your default response.

Why It Works:

- **Psychologically:** It disrupts the unconscious loop before it gathers momentum.
- **Neurologically:** The brain can't run the old pathway while you're consciously engaging a new one.
- **Spiritually:** Declaring "Cancel. Reset. Redirect." is like sending Spirit a correction, ensuring that only aligned energy is carried forward.

Key Insight: Pattern interrupts are your emergency brakes. The faster you use them, the quicker you steer your energy back onto the path of conscious creation.

Visualization Upgrade

Your imagination is one of the most powerful manifestation tools you have — but it can work for or against you. If you constantly picture worst-case scenarios, your brain and Spirit respond to those images as if they are instructions. Over time, this "negative rehearsal" strengthens fear and limits possibilities.

The good news: you can **upgrade** your visualization anytime. By deliberately picturing the best-case version, you retrain your brain to expect possibility rather than disaster.

How to Practice a Visualization Upgrade:

1. **Notice the Negative Image**
   Catch yourself when your mind begins to play out fears:

   - Seeing yourself failing an interview.
   - Imagine a fight with your partner.
   - Rehearsing a financial crisis.

2. **Pause and Interrupt**
   Acknowledge it without judgment: *"That was a worst-case picture. Cancel."*

3. **Paint the Best-Case Scenario**
   Close your eyes and deliberately imagine the outcome you want:

   - Instead of failing the interview → visualize yourself calm, confident, shaking hands, and receiving the job offer.
   - Instead of arguing with your partner → see yourselves communicating openly, finding understanding, and embracing afterward.
   - Instead of financial struggle → imagine opening your account and finding more than enough, or receiving unexpected income.

4. **Add Sensory Detail**
   Engage all your senses: what do you see, hear, smell, touch, and feel in the best-case outcome? The richer the detail, the more convincing it becomes for your subconscious.

5. **Anchor With Emotion**
   Feel the joy, relief, or gratitude as though it's already real. Emotion supercharges visualization, sending a stronger signal to both your brain and Spirit.

6. **Repeat Regularly**
   Every time a negative image arises, upgrade it. With

practice, your mind begins to default to possibility instead of limitation.

Why It Works:

- **Psychologically:** It redirects your focus toward solutions instead of problems.
- **Neurologically:** Neurons that fire together wire together — the more you imagine success, the stronger that pathway becomes.
- **Spiritually:** Spirit responds to the energy of belief. By holding the best-case vision, you invite alignment with outcomes that uplift and support you.

Key Insight: Your imagination is a rehearsal space for reality. Upgrade the script, and you upgrade the manifestation.

Affirmations with Emotion

Affirmations are more than words — they are instructions to your subconscious and signals to Spirit. But if you repeat them mechanically, without emotion or belief, they lose much of their power. The secret is not just to say the words, but to **feel** them as though they are already true.

How to Infuse Emotion into Your Affirmations:

1. **Slow Down and Breathe**
   Before speaking an affirmation, pause and take a deep breath. Center yourself so you're not just rushing through words. Presence amplifies impact.
2. **Engage Your Body**
   Place a hand on your heart, your belly, or another area that feels connected. This anchors the affirmation into your body, making it a full sensory experience rather than only mental.

3. **Visualize the Feeling**
Don't just say *"I am abundant."* Imagine what abundance feels like:

- The relief of paying bills with ease.
- The joy of giving generously.
- The excitement of seeing new opportunities flow your way.

4. **Use Emotional Language**
Add words that stir your spirit:

- Instead of: *"I am successful."*
- Try: *"I am joyfully successful, and I love the freedom it brings me."*

5. **Speak With Conviction**
Say it with the tone of someone who knows it's true. Confidence carries frequency — your subconscious and Spirit respond to authority, not hesitation.

6. **Amplify With Gratitude**
Close each affirmation by saying *"Thank you."* Gratitude bridges the gap between wanting and receiving, sealing the energy as if it has already arrived.

Example:

- Mechanical: *"I am abundant. I am abundant. I am abundant."*
- Embodied: (Hand on heart, eyes closed, deep breath) *"I am abundant. I feel abundance flowing through my life. I am grateful for the wealth of opportunities that surround me."*

Why It Works:

- **Psychologically:** Emotionally charged statements are more memorable and believable to the subconscious mind.
- **Neurologically:** Emotion activates the limbic system, strengthening new neural pathways tied to your affirmation.
- **Spiritually:** Spirit responds not only to words, but to the vibration of your energy. Feeling the affirmation broadcasts a clearer, stronger signal.

Key Insight: Words are the seed, but emotion is the water. Without feeling, affirmations stay flat. With feeling, they come alive and call your desires into form.

Healing Work

Sometimes negative thoughts aren't just passing worries — they are rooted in deep, unresolved wounds. Old traumas, limiting beliefs, or painful experiences can leave an imprint on your subconscious, shaping how you see yourself and what you believe is possible. This is why unconscious sabotage often feels so stubborn: it isn't about the present moment, but about the past still echoing in your energy field.

When old wounds remain unhealed, they can hijack your manifestations. Fear whispers, *"Don't try, you'll fail."* Shame says, *"You don't deserve it."* Abandonment warns, *"If you succeed, you'll lose love."* These hidden voices sabotage your goals before they even have a chance to grow.

Healing work dissolves the root causes, clearing space for new creation.

Ways to Heal at the Root:

- **Energy Healing:** Modalities such as Reiki, BodyTalk, EFT (tapping), Touch for Health, or auric clearing help release stuck emotions and rebalance the energy body. They bypass the conscious mind and shift what is held in the subconscious and nervous system.
- **Therapy or Counseling:** Talking through trauma or long-held beliefs can uncover patterns you may not see on your own. Therapists provide tools for rewiring thoughts and building healthier responses.
- **Spiritual Practices:** Prayer, meditation, and connection with Spirit create space for divine guidance and comfort. These practices lift you beyond the wound, helping you anchor into a higher truth of who you are.
- **Somatic Work:** Practices like breathwork, yoga, or trauma release exercises help clear stored stress and fear from the body itself, where it often hides.

Signs You May Need Healing Work:

- The same negative pattern keeps repeating, no matter what you try.
- Affirmations and visualization feel blocked or hollow.
- Fear or resistance shows up the moment you get close to your goal.
- Your body reacts strongly (tight chest, anxiety, stomach knots) when you think about your desire.

Key Insight: Healing work doesn't erase your past — it transforms it into wisdom. By clearing the roots of unconscious sabotage, you free your mind and Spirit to create without being dragged backward by old fears.

INTEGRATION PRACTICES: LIVING THE DREAM EVERY DAY

The true power of manifestation lies not in one big breakthrough, but in the small, consistent practices that keep you aligned. The DREAM Method is most effective when it becomes a rhythm in your daily life — a way of noticing, choosing, acting, and reflecting.

Here are two simple ways to anchor the method into your routine:

MORNING RITUAL: 10-MINUTE DREAM ALIGNMENT

Each morning, before you rush into the day, pause to align yourself with the cycle of creation.

1. **Drift** – Sit quietly for one minute. Notice what thoughts naturally float through your mind. Which ones feel light, exciting, or expansive?
2. **Recognize** – Choose one thought to hold. Write it down or say it aloud as your focus for the day.
3. **Execute** – Identify one small action you can take today to nurture that thought.
4. **Achieve** – Close your eyes and visualize yourself at the end of the day, feeling gratitude as if it is already done.
5. **Master** – Affirm: *"I live the DREAM today. I am open, aligned, and guided."*

This practice takes only a few minutes but sets the tone for the day ahead.

EVENING PRACTICE: REFLECTION JOURNAL

Before bed, take five minutes to reflect on the day and record your insights. Use the DREAM prompts to guide you:

- **Drift:** What drift-thoughts showed up today? Were there subtle whispers I almost ignored?
- **Recognize:** Which thoughts did I choose to focus on? Did they feel aligned?
- **Execute:** What actions did I take today that supported my intentions?
- **Achieve:** What small manifestations appeared today? (Even a parking space or a good conversation counts.)
- **Master:** What did I learn from today's cycle? How can I refine my focus tomorrow?

This practice closes the loop daily, training your subconscious to see manifestation as a natural, ongoing process.

By weaving the DREAM Method into both your mornings and evenings, you create a steady current of awareness, action, and reflection. Over time, this rhythm will make manifestation second nature — not something you have to *remember to do*, but something you naturally *are.*

MEDITATION EXERCISE: THE DREAM MANIFESTATION JOURNEY

Make yourself comfortable…
Take a slow, deep breath in… hold it for a moment… and exhale fully…
With each breath, allow yourself to sink deeper into stillness and ease…

As you read this…notice your toes… gently wiggle them… release any tension there…
Relax your ankles, calves, and knees…
Breathe into your thighs and hips… letting them grow heavy and relaxed…
Release your stomach and back…
Relax your shoulders, arms, and hands…
Take another deep breath into your chest… and exhale slowly…
Now soften your neck, your jaw, your face, even the space around your eyes…
Your entire body is calm, peaceful, open… ready to create.

…

Now imagine yourself standing in a tranquil garden…
The air is warm and soothing…
Birdsong echoes softly in the distance…
This garden is your inner world — the sacred space where manifestation begins.

Here, you begin the DREAM journey.

Step 1—D: Drift

In the palm of your hand, you notice a small, weightless spark — like a drifting seed.
This seed represents the unconscious thought, the whisper of possibility, planted without effort.

It floats to you gently, reminding you that every manifestation begins here — subtle, fleeting, yet full of potential.
Hold this seed lightly and let it rest in the soil of your imagination.

Step 2—R: Recognize

As you gaze at the soil, the seed begins to stir...
A tiny sprout emerges, reaching toward the light.
This is recognition — the moment you choose to notice and nurture the thought.
See yourself focusing on it with clarity, intention, and love.
Feel the joy of possibility as you commit to helping it grow.

Step 3—E: Execute

Now imagine yourself tending the sprout.
You water it, give it sunlight, shield it from harm.
These are your actions in the physical world — small, consistent, deliberate.
Every step you take tells Spirit: *"I am serious. I am ready."*
Notice how the sprout grows stronger with every choice aligned to your intention.

Step 4—A: Achieve

Before your eyes, the sprout transforms...
It blossoms into a vibrant flower, full and alive.
This flower is your manifestation — the desire made real.
Step closer... breathe in its fragrance... touch its petals... admire its beauty.
Feel gratitude rising in your heart as you realize: *"This is mine. I am living it."*

Step 5—M: Master

Now gently sit beside the flower...
Close your eyes and reflect: *What has this manifestation taught me?*
Do I want to repeat it, release it, or refine it?
Listen for Spirit's whisper — it may arrive as words, feelings, or a quiet knowing.
Breathe deeply and honor the wisdom received.
This is mastery: the ability to grow, refine, and evolve with each creation.

Now imagine the entire garden glowing with golden light...
Every seed, sprout, and flower around you represents the endless possibilities waiting for you.
You realize manifestation is not magic — it is a method.
A rhythm.
A partnership between your thoughts, your actions, Spirit, and your reflections.

Take one last deep breath...
Feel gratitude filling your heart...
And silently affirm:
"I live the DREAM: Drift, Recognize, Execute, Achieve, Master.
I co-create my reality with Spirit, for my highest good and best interest."

...

Slowly bring your awareness back to your body...
Wiggle your toes...
Stretch your arms...
And when you are ready, gently open your eyes...
Carrying with you the peace, clarity, and power of **The DREAM Method.**

MEDITATION EXERCISE: STEPPING INTO YOUR POWER AS CREATOR

Find a quiet place where you can be undisturbed...
Take three deep breaths...
With every inhale, draw in peace and clarity...
With every exhale, release tension, fear, and doubt...
Let your body grow heavy, yet your spirit grow light...

...

As you read this... imagine a golden light above your head...
It begins to flow down, washing gently over you...
Relax your forehead, your jaw, your shoulders...
Feel this golden light moving down through your chest, arms, and hands...
Through your hips, legs, and feet...
Until you are completely bathed in radiant, loving light.

This is the light of Spirit.
This is the energy of creation itself.
It has always been with you. It has never left you.

...

In this sacred space, you remember who you are...
You are not just someone who dreams — you are someone who creates.
Every thought you think plants a seed...
Every choice you make waters the garden of your life...
Every reflection you carry forward shapes your future harvest.

...

See yourself now standing in front of a vast, open field...
This is the field of infinite possibility...
Stretching far beyond what the eye can see.

In your hand, you hold seeds. Each seed is a desire, a dream, a vision for your life.
Some are small — simple, joyful wishes…
Others are great and bold — calling you into your highest purpose.

Spirit whispers: *"What you plant, I will help you grow."*

Take a deep breath… and choose one seed that matters to you now…
Place it in the soil with love…
Cover it gently, and press your hand to the earth…
Feel the pulse of life as the seed begins to awaken.

…

Now imagine this seed growing…
A sprout pushing through the soil…
Leaves stretching toward the sun…
A stem rising strong and tall…
Until, before you, stands the full bloom of your manifestation.

Look at it with awe.
Touch it with reverence.
This is not imagination — this is creation.
This is what happens when thought becomes energy, and energy becomes form.

…

Now step into the flower, as though it is a doorway…
On the other side, you are living your desire fully…
Feel the joy, the gratitude, the freedom of it…
See yourself thriving, smiling, at peace…
Let that emotion fill every cell of your body.

Anchor this truth within you: *"I am capable. I am worthy. I am powerful. I am a creator."*

...

And now, Spirit whispers again:
"Remember, what you manifest is not magic. It is your birthright.
Ask, and you shall receive. Act, and it shall be given form.
Reflect, and it shall bring wisdom.
You are never separate from Me. Together, we create."

Take a final deep breath, inhaling this truth...
And as you exhale, let go of any last remnants of fear or limitation.

When you are ready, wiggle your toes... move your fingers...
Return gently to the present moment...
And open your eyes — carrying the deep knowing that you are a conscious creator,
living the DREAM Manifestation Method with clarity, power, and grace.

Meditation: The DREAM Wealth Journey

Make yourself comfortable…
Close your eyes and take a deep, slow breath in…
Hold it gently… and exhale fully…
With each breath, release tension, letting your body sink into stillness.

Notice your toes… relax them…
Soften your ankles, calves, and knees…
Release your thighs and hips…
Breathe into your stomach and back…
Relax your shoulders, arms, and hands…
Take another deep breath into your chest… let it go…
Soften your neck, jaw, and face…
Your whole body is now calm, safe, and open to receive.

…

Imagine yourself standing in a golden garden — the garden of abundance.
The air glimmers with possibility…
The ground beneath you is fertile with wealth, ready to bring forth your desires.

Here, you begin the DREAM journey to manifest wealth.

D – Drift

See a golden seed resting in your hand.
This seed is a drift-thought — a fleeting whisper of wealth that your unconscious has carried: the wish for more ease, freedom, and flow.
Even if you've ignored it before, Spirit has heard it.
Feel this seed glow in your palm, carrying the energy of abundance.
Gently place it into the soil of your imagination.

R – Recognize

As you focus, the golden seed begins to sprout.
This is recognition — you are choosing to notice and nurture your desire for wealth.
See the sprout rising toward the light, and with it, feel clarity forming in your heart.
Say to yourself silently:
"I recognize my worth. I recognize my right to abundance."

E – Execute

Now see yourself tending to this sprout.
You water it, give it sunlight, and protect it.
Each action represents a step you can take in the real world — saving, investing, learning, creating, sharing your gifts.
Feel the energy of responsibility, alignment, and discipline flow through you.
Affirm:
"My actions align with abundance. Spirit sees that I am ready."

A – Achieve

Before your eyes, the sprout blossoms into a radiant golden tree…
Its branches are heavy with coins, its leaves shimmer like jewels, its roots are deep in the earth of infinite supply.
Step closer… touch the bark… feel its energy of stability and wealth.
Notice coins falling into your hands — your manifestation alive, your wealth real.
Smile and affirm:
"I achieve prosperity. I am living in abundance."

M – Master

Now sit beside the golden tree and reflect.
Ask yourself: *What does wealth mean to me?*
Is it freedom? Security? Opportunity? The ability to give?
Let Spirit whisper the answer.
Feel gratitude for this manifestation, and commit to refining your wealth mindset with wisdom, generosity, and purpose.
Affirm:
"I master the flow of wealth. I grow, refine, and evolve with abundance."

Now see the golden garden expand around you.
Everywhere you look, trees, flowers, and streams of abundance flow endlessly.
You realize that wealth is not outside of you — it flows through you, from seed to sprout to bloom.

Take a final deep breath and affirm silently:
"I live the DREAM: Drift, Recognize, Execute, Achieve, Master.
Wealth flows to me, through me, and for my highest good."

...

Slowly bring your awareness back to your body…
Wiggle your fingers and toes…
Stretch your arms…
And when you are ready, gently open your eyes…
Carrying with you the peace, clarity, and energy of abundance.

Meditation: The DREAM Health Journey

Make yourself comfortable…
Close your eyes and take a deep breath in…
Hold it gently… and exhale slowly…
With each breath, feel your body softening, relaxing, and
opening to healing.

Notice your toes… relax them…
Release your ankles, calves, and knees…
Soften your thighs and hips…
Breathe into your stomach and back, letting go of tension…
Relax your shoulders, arms, and hands…
Take another deep breath into your chest, exhale fully…
Soften your neck, jaw, and face…
Your body is now at ease, receptive, and ready to heal.

…

Now imagine yourself in a radiant garden of wellness.
The air feels fresh, clean, and vibrant…
Every breath fills you with life-force energy.
This is your inner sanctuary of health, where balance and
vitality are restored.

Here, you begin the DREAM journey.

D – Drift

See a small, glowing seed in your hand.
This seed is a drift-thought of health — the quiet wish for more
energy, balance, and wholeness.
Even if you've overlooked it before, Spirit has always heard it.
Place the glowing seed into the fertile soil of your imagination.

R – Recognize

As you focus, the seed begins to sprout.
This is recognition — the moment you choose to notice your
body's wisdom and honor your desire for health.
See the sprout reaching toward the light, growing stronger as
your awareness deepens.
Affirm silently:
*"I recognize my body's ability to heal. I honor my health with
love and care."*

E – Execute

Now see yourself tending to the sprout.
You water it, nourish it, and protect it.
Each action represents your real-world steps: eating well,
moving your body, resting, seeking care, and practicing self-
love.
Feel the energy of alignment and commitment flowing through
you.
Affirm:
*"My actions nurture my health. Spirit knows I am ready to
thrive."*

A – Achieve

Before your eyes, the sprout blossoms into a radiant tree of life,
pulsing with vibrant energy.
Golden light flows from its branches into your body —
restoring, renewing, revitalizing every cell.
Feel strength in your muscles, clarity in your mind, vitality in
your spirit.
Affirm:
*"I achieve radiant health. My body is alive with balance and
vitality."*

M – Master

Now sit beside the tree of life and reflect.
Ask yourself: *What has this journey toward health taught me?*
Is it patience, self-care, discipline, gratitude?
Let Spirit whisper the answer.
Feel gratitude for your body and its wisdom.
Affirm:
"I master my health by listening, learning, and evolving in harmony with Spirit."

Now see the entire garden glowing with healing light…
Every breath fills you with renewal… every heartbeat echoes with strength.
You realize that health is not outside of you — it flows through you, from thought to action to lived reality.

Take a final deep breath and affirm:
**"I live the DREAM: Drift, Recognize, Execute, Achieve, Master.
I am healthy, whole, and aligned with Spirit for my highest good."**

…

Slowly bring your awareness back to your body…
Wiggle your fingers and toes…
Stretch your arms…
And when you are ready, gently open your eyes…
Carrying with you peace, vitality, and the power of healing.

Meditation: The DREAM Happiness Journey

Find a comfortable position…
Close your eyes and take a deep breath in…
Hold it gently… and exhale slowly…
With each breath, let tension dissolve and lightness return.

Notice your toes and relax them…
Soften your ankles, calves, and knees…
Release your thighs and hips…
Breathe into your stomach and back, letting them loosen…
Relax your shoulders, arms, and hands…
Take another deep breath into your chest, then exhale
completely…
Soften your neck, jaw, and face…
Your body is now calm, open, and ready to welcome happiness.

…

Imagine yourself stepping into a radiant garden of joy.
The air feels fresh and playful…
You hear laughter carried by the breeze…
Warm sunlight pours over you, filling every part of your being.

Here, you begin the DREAM journey to manifest happiness.

D – Drift

In your hand appears a small glowing seed, light as air.
This seed is a drift-thought of happiness — the wish for joy,
laughter, and ease.
Even if you've overlooked it before, Spirit has always heard it.
Place the glowing seed into the fertile soil of your imagination.

R – Recognize

As you focus, the seed stirs and a sprout emerges.
This is recognition — the moment you choose to see happiness as your birthright, not a distant wish.
Watch it reach toward the light, stronger with every heartbeat of joy you allow in.
Affirm silently:
"I recognize happiness within me. Joy is mine to nurture."

E – Execute

Now see yourself tending to the sprout — watering it, giving it sunlight, protecting it.
These are your daily choices: gratitude, kindness, playfulness, surrounding yourself with uplifting people, and savoring small pleasures.
Every act nourishes your joy.
Affirm:
"My choices create happiness. Spirit knows I am ready to live in joy."

A – Achieve

Before your eyes, the sprout blossoms into a radiant flower, shining with colors of joy.
Step closer, breathe in its fragrance, and feel its laughter ripple through your body.
Smile as joy spreads through your heart, filling you with warmth and freedom.
Affirm:
"I achieve true happiness. My life is filled with lightness, laughter, and love."

M – Master

Now sit beside the flower and reflect.
Ask yourself: *What has this manifestation of happiness taught me?*
Is it gratitude, presence, simplicity, or the courage to let go?
Listen for Spirit's whisper.
Affirm:
"I master happiness by returning to joy, again and again."

Now see the entire garden glowing with golden light.
Everywhere you look are blossoms of joy — laughter, love, and peace rising from the soil of your soul.
You realize happiness is not something to chase — it grows within you, nurtured by thought, action, and Spirit.

Take one last deep breath and affirm:
"I live the DREAM: Drift, Recognize, Execute, Achieve, Master.
Happiness flows through me, now and always, for my highest good."

...

Slowly return your awareness to your body...
Wiggle your fingers and toes...
Stretch your arms...
And when you are ready, gently open your eyes...
Carrying with you the lightness, laughter, and joy of happiness.

Meditation: The DREAM Love Journey

Make yourself comfortable…
Close your eyes and take a deep, calming breath in…
Hold it gently… and exhale slowly…
With each breath, allow tension to melt away, leaving only openness.

Relax your toes… ankles… calves… and knees…
Soften your thighs and hips…
Breathe into your stomach and back, releasing any heaviness…
Relax your shoulders, arms, and hands…
Take another deep breath into your chest… let it out slowly…
Now soften your neck, jaw, and face…
Your whole body is peaceful, calm, and ready to welcome love.

…

Imagine yourself in a beautiful garden of roses and blossoms.
The air is warm and fragrant with sweetness.
Gentle light surrounds you, reminding you that love is always near.

Here, you begin the DREAM journey to manifest love.

D – Drift

See a delicate seed of light resting in your palm.
This seed is a drift-thought of love — the quiet wish to give and receive affection, connection, and belonging.
Even if you've overlooked it, Spirit has always heard it.
Place the glowing seed into the rich soil of your heart.

R – Recognize

As you focus, the seed begins to sprout.
This is recognition — the moment you honor your desire for love.
See the sprout reaching upward, vibrant with possibility.
Affirm silently:
"I recognize that I am worthy of love. Love flows to me and through me."

E – Execute

Now tend to the sprout with care — watering it, giving it sunlight, protecting it.
These are your actions in the world: speaking kindly, opening your heart, showing compassion, allowing yourself to connect.
Each act strengthens the roots of love in your life.
Affirm:
"My actions align with love. Spirit knows I am ready to give and receive deeply."

A – Achieve

Before your eyes, the sprout blossoms into a radiant rose, full and alive with beauty.
Step closer… breathe in its fragrance… feel love radiating into your body, wrapping you in warmth and tenderness.
See yourself embraced by love — whether through a partner, friendships, family, or self-love.
Affirm:
"I achieve love in all its forms. I am surrounded, supported, and cherished."

M – Master

Now sit beside the rose and reflect.
Ask yourself: *What has this manifestation of love taught me?*
Is it patience, openness, trust, or the courage to be vulnerable?
Let Spirit whisper the answer.
Affirm:
"I master love by living it daily — giving, receiving, and growing in its truth."

Now see the entire garden glowing with radiant light.
Every flower represents a different form of love: romantic, familial, friendship, spiritual, and self-love.
You realize love is not something outside of you — it blossoms within and extends outward, endlessly.

Take one final deep breath and affirm:
"I live the DREAM: Drift, Recognize, Execute, Achieve, Master.
I am love. I give love. I receive love. For my highest good and the highest good of all."

...

Slowly bring your awareness back to your body…
Wiggle your toes…
Stretch your arms…
And when you are ready, gently open your eyes…
Carrying with you the warmth, connection, and beauty of love.

Meditation: The DREAM Object Journey

Make yourself comfortable…
Close your eyes and take a deep breath in…
Hold it gently… and exhale slowly…
With every breath, release tension and open your mind to possibility.

Relax your toes and feet…
Soften your ankles, calves, and knees…
Release your thighs and hips…
Breathe into your stomach and back, letting go of heaviness…
Relax your shoulders, arms, and hands…
Take another deep breath into your chest and exhale fully…
Soften your neck, jaw, and face…
Your whole body is now calm, peaceful, and ready to create.

…

Imagine yourself standing in a clear, open space — a space where anything can appear.
This is the canvas of your imagination, where thought becomes form.

Here, you begin the DREAM journey to manifest your desired object.

D – Drift

Notice a small, glowing seed in your hand.
This seed represents the unconscious drift-thought of your object — the house, the car, the trip, or whatever you long for.
Even before you fully noticed it, Spirit did.
Place the seed into the soil of your imagination.

R – Recognize

As you focus, the seed begins to sprout.
This is recognition — the moment you choose to bring your desire into conscious awareness.
Picture the object clearly: the details, the colors, the feeling it brings you.
Affirm silently:
"I recognize my desire, and I welcome it into my life."

E – Execute

Now see yourself tending to the sprout — watering it, protecting it, giving it sunlight.
These are your actions in the real world: researching, planning, saving, aligning your energy with the object.
Each step strengthens the roots of your manifestation.
Affirm:
"My actions align with my desire. Spirit sees I am ready."

A – Achieve

Before your eyes, the sprout transforms into your object, fully formed.
If it is a house — see yourself opening the door and stepping inside.
If it is a car — see yourself sliding into the seat and starting the engine.
If it is a trip — see yourself walking the streets, the beaches, or the mountains of your destination.
Feel the joy and gratitude in your body as if it is already yours.
Affirm:
"I achieve my desire. It is here. It is mine."

M – Master

Now sit beside your manifestation and reflect.
Ask yourself: *What has this manifestation taught me?*
Is it patience, trust, action, or faith?
Listen for Spirit's whisper.
Affirm:
"I master creation by reflecting, refining, and opening to more."

Now see the entire space around you fill with glowing objects — endless possibilities ready to be manifested in your life. You realize manifestation is not random — it is a cycle, a method, a partnership between your thoughts, actions, Spirit, and reflection.

Take a final deep breath and affirm:
**"I live the DREAM: Drift, Recognize, Execute, Achieve, Master.
My desires flow into reality, for my highest good and best interest."**

...

Slowly bring your awareness back to your body...
Wiggle your fingers and toes...
Stretch your arms...
And when you are ready, gently open your eyes...
Carrying with you the clarity and confidence that your object is already on its way.

Meditation: Releasing Blocks

Find a comfortable position…
Take a slow, deep breath in…
Hold it gently… and exhale fully…
With each breath, allow your body to soften and your mind to open.

…

As you read this…imagine yourself standing before a beautiful doorway. This doorway leads to your goal — the desire you want to manifest. The dream is glowing brightly on the other side, calling to you with warmth and excitement.

But in front of the doorway are a few stones — these represent the blocks in your path. They may be doubts, fears, limiting beliefs, lack of clarity, or outside obstacles. Whatever they are, allow one stone to come into focus.

Gently pick up the stone. Hold it in your hands. Feel its weight. Notice what word or feeling comes with it. Perhaps it says: *fear… unworthy… not enough time… not enough money…* Whatever arises, trust it.

Now take a deep breath in… and as you exhale, imagine golden light flowing from your heart into the stone. The stone begins to grow warm and lighter, dissolving into shimmering particles of energy. You whisper:
"I see you. I thank you. I release you now."

The block melts away, leaving space for possibility.

…

Another stone calls to your attention. Pick it up. Notice what it represents. Perhaps it is doubt, procrastination, the opinions of

others. Acknowledge it fully. Breathe golden light into it.
Watch it dissolve as you affirm:
*"I choose clarity. I choose freedom. I choose alignment with
Spirit."*

. . .

Now look at the doorway again. Fewer stones remain. With
each breath, continue this process — recognizing a block,
holding it with compassion, and dissolving it into light. One by
one, the path clears.

When the last stone is gone, the doorway stands open. Brilliant
light pours through. Step forward now, through the doorway,
into your dream. Feel yourself living it — the joy, the ease, the
gratitude. It is already real.

Take a deep breath and affirm silently:
**"My path is clear. I am ready. I live the DREAM for my
highest good and the highest good of all."**

. . .

Slowly return to your body. Wiggle your fingers and toes. Take
a gentle stretch. When you are ready, open your eyes —
carrying with you the freedom and clarity of a clear path.

Common Manifestation Blocks

- Lack of clarity (not sure what you really want)
- Conflicting desires (wanting two opposing things at once)
- Doubt in yourself
- Doubt in Spirit / the process
- Fear of failure
- Fear of success
- Fear of judgment from others
- Fear of responsibility or change
- Negative self-talk ("I'm not worthy," "I can't do this")
- Old limiting beliefs from childhood or society
- Unhealed trauma or emotional wounds
- Guilt about wanting more
- Feeling unworthy of receiving
- Lack of time or energy
- Lack of money or resources
- Lack of skills or knowledge
- Procrastination
- Perfectionism
- Impatience (wanting results too quickly)
- Past disappointments create resistance
- Overthinking or over-analyzing
- Dependence on others' approval
- Toxic relationships are draining energy
- Chaotic or unsupportive environment
- Carrying responsibility for others' happiness
- Not trusting intuition
- Attachment to old stories or identities
- Forgetting to take aligned action
- Refusing to release what no longer serves you

Manifesting with Responsibility and Grace

MANIFESTING FOR COMMUNITY AND WORLD HEALING

Manifestation is often thought of in personal terms — a new job, a home, a relationship, or financial ease. Yet, the same process that shapes your individual life can also be used for the collective good. When you focus your thoughts, actions, and reflections on healing for others, you contribute to a greater field of possibility that Spirit responds to.

Why Collective Manifestation Matters

- **Shared Energy Amplifies:** When many people hold the same vision of healing, peace, or justice, the energy multiplies. This is why prayer circles, global meditations, and community intentions feel so powerful.
- **Ripple Effect:** Every manifestation that lifts you also lifts those around you. When you create love, abundance, and peace in your own life, it radiates outward.
- **Partnership with Spirit:** Spirit always honors intentions for the highest good. When you manifest beyond yourself, you align deeply with that universal flow.

How to Apply the DREAM Method Collectively

- **Drift:** Notice the subtle worries or wishes you have about your community or the world — these are seeds of collective care.
- **Recognize:** Choose one area you feel called to focus on: environmental healing, social justice, peace, or health. Hold it clearly in your awareness.

- **Execute:** Take aligned action, no matter how small — volunteer, donate, share knowledge, or simply send daily prayer or loving energy.
- **Achieve:** Celebrate the visible shifts, even small ones — a community event that uplifts, a law that changes, a person who finds hope.
- **Master:** Reflect on what your contribution taught you, and refine your vision for even greater impact.

Practice: A Simple World-Healing Meditation

Sit quietly, breathe deeply, and bring to mind an image of the Earth glowing in golden light. Imagine this light flowing into areas of conflict, illness, or pain, bringing healing and renewal. Whisper silently:
"May peace, love, and balance manifest for the highest good of all."

By manifesting for the collective, you remember that the DREAM Method is not only about personal fulfillment but about co-creating a world where everyone has the chance to thrive.

COLLECTIVE MANIFESTATIONS: THE POWER OF SHARED BELIEF

When more than one person focuses on the same vision, the energy magnifies. Shared belief accelerates manifestation because thoughts are not isolated — they ripple into the collective field of consciousness. Spirit responds not only to individual desires, but also to the harmonized intentions of many.

Why Shared Belief Works

- **Amplified Energy:** A single thought is a spark; a group of thoughts becomes a flame. The more minds aligned with the same vision, the stronger the signal.
- **Collective Permission:** When multiple people agree on a possibility, resistance weakens. The group begins to normalize the belief that "this can happen," making it easier to anchor in reality.
- **Historic Proof:** Consider how humanity once believed the earth was flat — until enough people believed in exploration and proved otherwise. Shared belief reshaped our world. The same principle applies to modern breakthroughs, inventions, and social change.

How to Use the DREAM Method Collectively

- **Drift:** Notice the shared longings present in conversations, communities, or global movements.
- **Recognize:** Clarify a collective vision — peace, healing, justice, innovation — and hold it with intention.
- **Execute:** Take aligned action as a group — whether through community service, group meditation, advocacy, or shared affirmations.
- **Achieve:** Celebrate collective milestones together, no matter how small. Each achievement reinforces belief and accelerates momentum.
- **Master:** Reflect as a group. What worked? What shifted? How can the collective refine and strengthen the vision?

Practice: Shared Belief Affirmation

Gather with others (physically or virtually). Together, speak aloud an intention:
"We see it. We believe it. We welcome it into reality for the highest good of all."

Feel the resonance as voices merge — each word amplified, each heart aligned.

Collective manifestation is a reminder that you are never creating alone. Every thought contributes to the greater field. By joining your vision with others, you accelerate change not just for yourself, but for the world.

ETHICAL MANIFESTATION: THE 'HIGHEST GOOD' CLAUSE

Manifestation is powerful — and with power comes responsibility. When you set an intention, you are not only shaping your own life, you are also sending ripples into the lives of others. For this reason, it is essential to ground your practice in ethics.

One simple safeguard is to always add the clause:
"For my highest good and the highest good of all."

Why This Matters

- **Protects You from Harm:** Sometimes what you think you want may not truly serve you in the long run. By adding this clause, you allow Spirit to redirect your manifestation into something better aligned.
- **Respects Others' Free Will:** Manifestation should never be about controlling, coercing, or harming others. The highest good clause ensures your desire unfolds in harmony with others, not at their expense.
- **Aligns You with Spirit:** Spirit honors intentions that are rooted in growth, love, and balance. By setting boundaries of goodness, you keep your energy aligned with that universal flow.

Examples

- Instead of: *"I want that person to fall in love with me,"* shift to: *"I welcome love into my life, for my highest good and the highest good of all."*
- Instead of: *"I want to win at all costs,"* shift to: *"I welcome success that supports me and uplifts others."*

Reflection Prompt

Ask yourself: *If this manifestation arrives, how will it affect me, my relationships, and the world around me?*
If the answer uplifts, empowers, and expands — you are in alignment. If it diminishes, harms, or controls — it is time to refine.

Ethical manifestation keeps your desires rooted in integrity. It reminds you that true abundance is never taken from someone else — it flows from Spirit in ways that benefit all.

Chapter 7: Bringing It All Together

LIVING THE DREAM MANIFESTATION METHOD

Manifestation is not something that happens once in a while — it is happening all the time. Thoughts are constantly flowing, seeds are always being planted, and Spirit is always listening. The difference lies in whether you engage the process consciously or let it unfold unconsciously.

PLEASURE AND PAIN: THE MOTIVATION TO CHANGE

How bad does it have to get before you finally decide to change? For many people, the answer is: *very bad.* Pain often becomes the motivator when nothing else works. But it doesn't have to be this way. You can choose to change from a place of inspiration and desire, not just suffering.

Still, pain is a powerful teacher. It wakes us up. It shows us clearly what we no longer want. When the pain of staying the same becomes greater than the fear of change, transformation happens.

Resources for Change

There are countless paths available when you're ready to shift. Magazines, websites, trade shows, and community boards often list practitioners, courses, and seminars that can help.

- **Modalities:** meditation, hypnosis, counseling, energy healing, self-esteem, and self-improvement programs.
- **Where to Find Help:**
    - Health and healing sections of local directories.
    - Alternative practitioners in your area.
    - Health food stores or New Age shops often feature bulletin boards with listings of practitioners and upcoming events.
    - Books and online resources that offer practical tools for personal growth.

The Value of New Perspectives

I personally enjoy taking new courses because each one gives me another way to think, act, or create. Sometimes it's a gentle reminder, other times it's a "whammy" — a wake-up call that shakes me out of my patterns and forces me to move the inner garbage that's been blocking me. Both are valuable. Both serve the purpose of bringing me back on track.

From Impossible to Inevitable

Dreams often move through stages:

- At first they seem **impossible**.
- With time and exploration, they feel **improbable**.
- But once you summon the will, align your thoughts, and take action, they become **inevitable.**

Christopher Reeve said it best:

"So many of our dreams at first seem impossible, then they seem improbable, and when we summon the will, they soon become inevitable."

Key Insight: Pain may push you, but pleasure can pull you. The moment you decide you've had enough of one and deserve more of the other, manifestation accelerates.

DAILY PRACTICE

When you bring awareness to the DREAM steps — unconscious thought, conscious thought, preparation, manifestation, and reflection — manifestation becomes a daily practice rather than an occasional event. You begin to notice the flow everywhere:

- **Unconscious thought:** The quick flashes of desire that come and go.
- **Conscious thought:** The ones you choose to hold onto and revisit.
- **Preparation:** The actions, big or small, that move energy into form.
- **Manifestation:** The moment when desire becomes lived reality.
- **Reflection (+1):** The wisdom gained that shapes the next cycle.

START SMALL

The best way to train yourself is to notice the cycle in everyday experiences:

- Craving a cup of coffee and finding yourself drinking one minutes later.
- Wishing for a parking spot and watching one open up.

- Thinking of someone and receiving a text or call from them.

These small manifestations build your awareness and confidence. They show you that Spirit is always listening and that the cycle is always alive.

EXPAND TO BIGGER GOALS

Once you see the cycle in small things, begin to apply it to larger areas of your life:

- **Career:** Choosing the kind of work that fulfills you, preparing through learning and networking, and manifesting opportunities aligned with your purpose.
- **Relationships:** Shifting unconscious patterns, focusing on the qualities you desire in connection, and preparing your heart to welcome love.
- **Healing:** Holding a vision of health, taking aligned steps in care and self-nourishment, and reflecting on the lessons your body teaches you.

The process is the same, whether you are calling in a parking space or a new chapter of your life. What changes is the scale, the number of people involved, and the depth of alignment required.

THE POWER OF GOALS IN MANIFESTATION

Without goals, what are we truly living for? Goals give the mind a direction and Spirit a target. They are the blueprint that turns raw desire into form. As Scripture reminds us: *"Ask, and you shall receive."* But if we do not ask, Spirit has nothing to respond to.

DIAGRAM A: A PERSON WITH NO GOALS

When someone has not set goals, Spirit has no clear way to assist. Without focus, energy scatters, drifting into random outcomes rather than intentional creation. It is like planting seeds without ever deciding what garden you want to grow.

DIAGRAM B: THE WAVE OF GOALS OVER TIME

Most business and personal development courses encourage setting 1, 5, 10, and 20-year goals. This is wise, because life naturally moves in waves — good times and challenges, expansions and contractions.

1......... . . . .5...... . .... . .10......... . . .20

As you ride these waves, your goals serve as anchors. They remind you where you are going, even when life feels chaotic. Spirit uses these markers to align opportunities and guide you through both the highs and lows.

DIAGRAM C: THE "RETIREMENT GAP"

One common mistake is forgetting to set new goals once earlier ones are achieved. Many retired people find themselves in this situation — they worked toward the dream of retirement, achieved it, and then... nothing.

1.......·...5......·....10.......·...20....... and then nothing

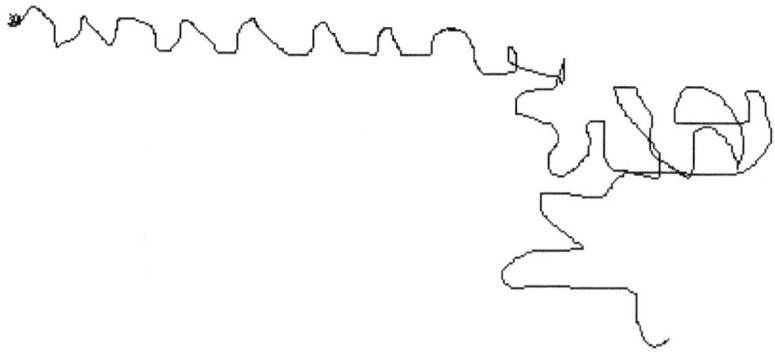

Without fresh goals, life can lose its sense of purpose. Spirit still listens, but with no requests being made, there is nothing to align or bring forth.

THE LESSON OF GOALS

If you do not ask, Spirit cannot help you achieve your goals. Goals don't just keep you busy — they keep you alive, inspired, and growing. They act as signposts for Spirit to guide your path.

Key Insight: Always have something before you, whether big or small. When one goal is achieved, set another. Spirit is limitless, but Spirit needs your clarity to respond.

EXERCISE: SETTING, TESTING, AND REFINING YOUR GOALS

Step 1: State Your Goal

Write down your goal in clear, affirmative language. (Refer to the *How to Write Affirmations* section in the appendix to ensure it is stated in the proper format.)

Step 2: Test Your Goal Through Reflection Questions

For the goal written above, answer the following questions. Be honest and specific. The more emotion tied to your answers, the more inner work you may need to do before your manifestation can flow.

1. How has achieving your goal affected your friendships? (Example: you see your old friends more/less, not at all, or you've gained new ones.)

---

2. How has achieving your goal affected your children?

---

3. How has achieving your goal affected your intimate relationship?

4. How has achieving your goal affected your money matters?

5. How has achieving your goal affected your spiritual/religious beliefs?

6. How has achieving your goal affected your self-esteem?

7. How has achieving your goal affected your health (sports, activities, food choices)?

Interpreting Your Answers:

- If you had **no emotional answers**, your goal is aligned, and manifestation can happen quickly.
- If you had **several emotional answers**, your subconscious is signaling potential obstacles. These must be cleared before your manifestation will fully take root.

Consider working with a counselor (holistic or traditional), hypnotherapist, or practitioners of Reiki, EFT, BodyTalk, Touch for Health, PKP/BKP, energy balancing, or emotional clearing methods to dissolve blocks.

Key Insight: Obstacles are not failures — they are solutions in disguise. Each obstacle shows you where alignment is needed.

Examples of Obstacles Becoming Solutions

- **Goal #1: A Horse**
  Obstacle: No money.
  Solution: A bank letter arrived, increasing a loan limit with a blank cheque, just enough to buy the horse.
- **Goal #2: A Couch**
  Obstacle: No money.
  Solution: A person dreamed of a new couch, then unexpectedly won enough money at the casino to buy one.
- **Goal #3: A House**
  Obstacle: Bank refusal.
  Solution: Another bank approved the loan.
- **Goal #4: A Different Car**
  Obstacle: Lease restrictions.
  Solution: The Dealer replaced the smelly leased car with a newer model after the person demanded a resolution.
- **Goal #5: Yellow Roses**
  Obstacle: Nature itself.
  Solution: A person bought one pot of red and one of yellow roses. After wishing for both to be yellow, both bloomed yellow.

Lesson: No matter what, your obstacle contains your solution. Spirit and your subconscious work together — sometimes rerouting, sometimes surprising you — but always responding to your focus.

WHAT MIGHT BE STOPPING YOU?

Sometimes it isn't the goal itself that's difficult — it's the hidden beliefs, fears, or circumstances standing in the way. This exercise helps you uncover what may be silently blocking your manifestations.

Step 1: Choose Your Goal
Think of a goal or dream you want to manifest. Hold it clearly in your mind and write it at the top of a page.

Step 2: Answer the Questions Honestly

1. **What will you gain from achieving your goal?**

---

2. **What is stopping you from achieving your dream today?**

---

3. **If you achieved your dream, who or what might it negatively affect?**
(Examples: Family, relationships, job, finances, lifestyle)

---

4. **How do your present situation, behaviors, or beliefs affect your long-term values or other goals?**
(Example: You want to travel, but you have a six-month-old child.)

---

5. **What emotion do you feel when you don't achieve your goal?**

Step 3: Notice the Pattern
When you read your answers, do you see recurring fears, excuses, or conflicts? These patterns reveal what needs healing or adjustment before Spirit can align the manifestation.

Step 4: Learn From Your Feelings
Sometimes your emotions give you the clearest answer. You can even use a tool like a coin flip — heads for *yes*, tails for *no*. But don't focus on the coin itself — notice how you *feel* about the result. If the answer is *no* and you feel relieved, then don't pursue it. If the answer is *no* and you feel upset, then the truth is you do want it.

Key Insight: An addict can only heal once they admit they are one. The same is true with manifestation — until you admit what's blocking you, you can't move forward. Awareness is the first step to freedom.

MANIFESTATION/CREATION EXPANSION EXERCISE

Write out **100 things you will accomplish before death.** This trains your mind to keep setting new goals, giving Spirit more opportunities to support you.

You can apply this to any area of life:

- **House Renovations:** Write down every detail, room by room.
- **Job or Career:** Be specific about income, environment, colleagues, flexibility, and fulfillment.
- **Perfect Mate:** List 100 qualities you desire (looks, hobbies, values, career, family, politics, addictions, etc.).

Rule of thumb: After dating someone for three months, if they do not meet at least 80% of your list, keep looking.

Key Insight: Spirit can only deliver what you clearly ask for. The more detailed and aligned your goals, the easier it is for manifestation to flow into your life.

The DREAM Action Plan: A Step-by-Step Exercise

0) Set yourself up (5 minutes)

- Grab a dedicated journal/notebook.
- Write the clause at the top of the first page:
  "For my highest good and the highest good of all."

1) Read & note (same day)

- Skim the book once; then reread **DREAM** chapters.
- Highlight one takeaway for each step:
  - **Drift • Recognize • Execute • Achieve • Master**

2) Write out your goals (solo or with a partner)

- **Brain dump (10 minutes):** list 20–100 things you'd love to create.
- **Group into themes:** health, wealth, love, home, purpose, creativity, service.
- **If working with a partner:** each writes a *personal* list first, then share and mark:
  - **Ours** (shared), **Mine, Yours, Later.**

3) Pick ONE focal goal for a 30-day cycle

- Choose the goal that is **meaningful + doable** in 30 days (a finish or a clear milestone).
- Write a one-sentence intention:
  "In 30 days, I will (milestone) for (goal)."

4) Run the goal through the DREAM Method

D — Drift Scan (2 minutes)

- What unconscious whispers have shown up about this goal lately?
- Capture 3 "drift-thoughts."

R — Recognize (5 minutes)

- Clarify the intention as a single, vivid sentence (present tense, positive, specific).
- Add the safeguard: **"…for my highest good and the highest good of all."**
- Define **success criteria** (how you'll know you've advanced in 30 days).

E — Execute (10 minutes)

- List **3 aligned actions** you can take this week (each ≤ 60 minutes).
- Circle **one "Minimum Viable Action"** you will do **today** (≤ 15 minutes).
- Put all three actions on your calendar.

A — Achieve (micro-wins)

- Track daily micro-evidence: emails sent, research done, workouts finished, dollars saved, pages written, etc.
- Celebrate every proof point (gratitude note, small reward).

M — Master (weekly)

- Each week, answer:
    - What worked?
    - What didn't?
    - What will I change next week?

- Reaffirm (or refine) the intention.

5) Diagnose what's blocking you (10-minute audit)

Rate 0–10 (low→high) for each item. Anything ≤ 6 is a likely block.

- **Clarity** (I know exactly what I want)
- **Belief** (I truly believe it's possible for me)
- **Safety** (It feels emotionally safe to succeed)
- **Skills/Knowledge** (I know how to do the next steps)
- **Time/Energy** (I have capacity)
- **Money/Resources** (I have or can access what's needed)
- **Support** (My environment/people support this)
- **Alignment** (It serves my values & highest good)

Circle the **lowest** scores—those are your priority blocks.

6) Fix it: targeted block-busters (choose what fits)

If the block is Clarity

- Rewrite the intention with **who/what/when/where/how much**.
- Create a 3-bullet **Outcome Picture** (how it looks, feels, functions).

If the block is a Belief / Limiting story

- Write the limiting thought → replace with a **truth-based** reframe.
  "I've never done this" → *"I'm learning; small wins prove progress."*
- Daily **embodied affirmation** (say it slowly, hand on heart, feel it).

If the block is Safety (fear/judgment)

- Make a **confidence ladder** (5 tiny exposures from easiest→hardest).
  Do rung #1 today.
- Boundary script: *"Thanks for caring; I'm committed to this next step."*

If the block is Skills/Knowledge

- Pick one **micro-course/mentor/resource** and schedule 2 sessions this week.
- Practice loop: **Learn 10 min → Do 20 min → Note 2 improvements.**

If the block is Time/Energy

- Timebox **15 minutes/day** (non-negotiable) for this goal.
- Swap one low-value habit for a high-value action.

If the block is Money/Resources

- Reduce scope to a **starter version**; list 3 alternative ways: borrow, rent, barter, free trial, scholarship, partner.
- Set a **savings target** and automate a small weekly transfer.

If the block is Support/Environment

- Curate inputs (unsubscribe/mute what drains).
- Add a **DREAM buddy**; send a 1-line progress text daily.

If the block is Alignment/Spirit

- Add the clause to every intention. Pray/meditate 3 minutes:
  "This or something better, in perfect timing, for the highest good."

If emotions keep spiking, consider healing support (therapy, EFT/tapping, Reiki, somatic work). Clearing the root accelerates everything.

7) Daily & Evening micro-rituals (≤ 10 minutes total)

Morning (5 minutes)

- 1-minute Drift notice → choose today's focus (Recognize).
- Name one 15-minute action (Execute).
- 20-second visualization of end-of-day success (Achieve).
- Quick affirmation (Master):
  "I live the DREAM today, for the highest good."

Evening (5 minutes)

- Journal:
  Drift I noticed → What I recognized → What I executed → What I achieved → Lesson for mastery.

8) Weekly check-in (20 minutes)

- Score progress (0–10) on **Clarity/Belief/Action/Evidence/Peace**.
- Celebrate 3 wins.
- Choose 1 tweak for next week.
- Renew intention with the **Highest Good** clause.

9) Partner pathway (if doing this with someone)

- Share individual goals, then co-create **One Shared Intention** for 30 days.
- Agree on **roles**, **budget/time**, and **3 joint actions** this week.
- Weekly "DREAM Together" chat (15 minutes): wins, lessons, next steps.
- Keep the mantra: **"Us vs. the problem, not us vs. each other."**

10) Example Only (fill-in)

Goal: *Book a 7-day Mexico trip within 90 days; 30-day milestone = deposit paid.*

- **D:** I keep picturing ocean sunsets.
- **R:** "We place the deposit for our Mexico trip within 30 days, for our highest good."
- **E (this week):** Price 3 resorts; request time-off dates; open travel fund.
- **A (micro-wins):** Found flight deal; friend recommended resort; PTO pre-approved.
- **M (lesson):** Tuesday planning works; need a backup date.

11) Reset ritual (when stuck—5 minutes)

- Breathe. Say: **"This is feedback, not failure."**
- Ask: *Where am I in DREAM? Which step needs love?*
- Take one **15-minute** action now.
- Reaffirm the clause: **"This or something better, in perfect timing."**

One-line commitment

"For the next 30 days, I will live the DREAM—Drift, Recognize, Execute, Achieve, Master—on one worthy goal, for my highest good and the highest good of all."

DREAM Method — Step-by-Step Journal Prompts

Deep-Dive (use when you start a new goal)

D — Drift (Unconscious Thought)

- What thoughts/feelings have been quietly "drifting" into my mind about this goal?
- What did I dream last night (or recently) that might relate? Symbols? Emotions?
- Where in my day do these thoughts arise (places, people, times)?
- If this desire were a **seed**, what quality does it carry (freedom, love, safety, creativity, service)?
- What would happen if I *ignored* this drift-thought for 6 months?

R — Recognize (Conscious Focus)

- What, exactly, am I choosing to focus on?
- One-sentence intention (present tense + specific + positive + time frame):
  "I ___ by/within ___, for my highest good and the highest good of all."
- Why does this matter to me now? (deeper value it serves)
- How will I know I'm on track? (3 measurable signals)

E — Execute (Aligned Action)

- List 3 **aligned actions** I can take this week (each ≤ 60 minutes).
- What is my **Minimum Viable Action** I can do **today** (≤ 15 minutes)?

- What resources do I already have? What do I need? (people, knowledge, money, tools)
- What will I put on my calendar, and when?

A — Achieve (Living It)

- If success were already true, what would today look like? (sensory details)
- What small wins would prove momentum? (emails sent, calls made, pages written…)
- How will I celebrate micro-evidence? (tiny reward, gratitude note)

M — Master (Reflect, Refine, Repeat)

- What worked? What didn't? What surprised me?
- What belief or habit changed this week?
- What will I do **differently** next week?
- Do I keep, release, or refine this goal? Why?

Daily Quick Log (5 minutes a day)

Morning

- Drift I notice right now:
- Today I **Recognize** (my focus is):
- One **Execute** step I will do today (≤ 15 min):
- Mini-visualization of **Achieve** (1–2 sentences):
- Mastery mantra: "I live the DREAM today, for my highest good and the highest good of all."

Evening

- Drift that appeared today:
- What I actually Recognized and protected my focus from:

- Action(s) Executed:
- Evidence/Achieve moments (synchronicities/wins):
- Master lesson (1 sentence) + tweak for tomorrow:

Weekly Review (20 minutes)

- On a 0–10 scale, rate: **Clarity** __ / Belief __ / Action __ / Evidence __ / Peace __
  → Lowest number is my focus next week.
- Top 3 wins:
- One obstacle I hit & what it taught me:
- Intention (updated if needed):
  "I ___ by/within ___, for my highest good and the highest good of all."
- Three actions scheduled for next week (dates/times):
- Keep • Release • Refine (circle one) — and why:

Block Audit (10 minutes)

Rate each 0–10 (low→high). Anything ≤ **6** is a likely block.

- Clarity (I know exactly what I want): __
- Belief (I trust it's possible for me): __
- Safety (It feels safe to succeed/change): __
- Skills/Knowledge (I know my next step): __
- Time/Energy (I have capacity): __
- Money/Resources (I have or can access what's needed): __
- Support/Environment (People/space help, not hinder): __
- Alignment/Spirit (Matches my values & highest good): __

For the lowest two scores, journal:

- The story I'm telling myself is…
- The truthful reframe is…
- One tiny action to lift this score by 1 point this week is…
- Help, I will seek (person/resource/practice):

Dream Capture (use on waking, ties to Drift)

- Fragments I remember:
- Strongest emotion:
- 1–3 symbols:
- Possible message about my goal:
- One action or question I'll carry into today:

Ethical Alignment (Highest Good)

- If this manifests, who/what is affected and how?
- How could this outcome uplift more than just me?
- Add the clause to my intention:
  "…for my highest good and the highest good of all."

Optional: Partner Prompts (if manifesting together)

- Our shared intention (one sentence):
- What matters most to **each** of us about this goal:
- Roles/commitments this week (who does what by when):
- Weekly "DREAM Together" check-in notes: wins, lessons, next steps.

- Our relationship boundary/upgrade we'll honor while we create this:

ONE-PAGE STARTER TEMPLATE (copy this into your journal)

Goal/Milestone (30 days):
Intention: "I ___ by/within ___, for my highest good and the highest good of all."

This Week

- E1:
- E2:
- E3:

Daily (Evening)

- Drift:
- Recognize:
- Execute:
- Achieve (evidence):
- Master (lesson → tweak):

Weekly Review

- Scores C/B/A/E/P: / /__ /__ /__
- Keep • Release • Refine:
- Next week's top 3 actions:

How to Use the One-Page Starter Template

This template is designed to keep your manifestation practice focused and simple. One page covers an entire week. Here's how to work with it:

Step 1: Set Your Goal (once every 30 days)

At the top of the page, write your **30-day milestone** — something meaningful but doable.
Example: *"Book a trip to Mexico by May 15."*

Then, write your **intention** in clear, present-tense language:
"I joyfully pay the deposit for my Mexico trip by May 15, for my highest good and the highest good of all."

Step 2: Plan Your Week (every Sunday or Monday)

Fill in your **3 main actions (E1, E2, E3)** that will move your goal forward this week. These should be practical and aligned. Example:

- E1: Research three travel agencies.
- E2: Talk with my friend about possible dates.
- E3: Create a savings plan for the trip.

Step 3: Capture Your Daily Practice (each evening)

Spend 3–5 minutes filling in the "Daily" section:

- **Drift:** What small, unconscious thoughts floated in today? (Positive or negative.)
- **Recognize:** What intention did I actually choose to focus on?
- **Execute:** What action did I take today toward my goal?
- **Achieve (evidence):** What signs, synchronicities, or wins showed up? (Even small ones — a recommendation, an ad, or a conversation count!)
- **Master (lesson → tweak):** What did I learn today, and how will I adjust tomorrow?

This builds awareness and keeps the DREAM cycle active.

Step 4: Weekly Review (end of the week)

Rate yourself on the **5 scales**:

- **C (Clarity)** – Did I stay clear on what I want?
- **B (Belief)** – Did I believe it's possible for me?
- **A (Action)** – Did I take consistent steps?
- **E (Evidence)** – Did I notice signs/results?
- **P (Peace)** – Did I stay in trust instead of stress?

Circle **Keep, Release, or Refine** for your goal.

- *Keep* = Still aligned, continue.
- *Release* = No longer serves, let it go.
- *Refine* = Adjust the focus or approach.

Finally, set your **top 3 actions for next week**.

Over 30 days, these weekly pages will show your progress, teach you where blocks appear, and help you refine until the goal is achieved.

Final Reflection

Manifestation is often mistaken for magic — something mysterious, mystical, and beyond our reach. But as you've now seen, it is neither random nor reserved for a select few. Manifestation is a **natural, repeatable process** built into the way Spirit, mind, and energy work together.

Every desire begins as a seed — an unconscious spark. When you choose to nurture it through conscious thought, prepare for it with action, live it in reality, and reflect on its lessons, you are engaging in a cycle as old as creation itself.

This is not wishful thinking. It is alignment. It is awareness. It is the practice of bringing the unseen into the seen, the imagined into the lived.

The **DREAM Manifestation Method** shows you that manifestation isn't luck or coincidence. It is a rhythm you can trust, repeat, and refine. Once you understand the steps, you begin to see them everywhere — in small daily desires like coffee, conversations, or parking spots, and in larger life goals like career, relationships, or healing.

Key Insight: Manifestation is not magic. It is the art of aligning thought, energy, action, and reflection with Spirit. And because it is a process, it can be practiced, strengthened, and mastered.

CAREFUL WHAT YOU WISH FOR

As you practice the DREAM Method, you may notice something surprising: your manifestations begin to arrive faster. At first, you might need to follow each step deliberately, but as your focus sharpens and your belief strengthens, Spirit begins to respond more quickly.

This is both exciting — and something to approach with care. Because the mind is powerful, even passing thoughts can sometimes take shape. That's why awareness and refinement (the **Master** step) are so important.

Why This Matters

- Stray, emotional thoughts can sometimes drift into reality.
- Manifestations may arrive before you've "finished" all five steps.
- Not every passing desire is truly in alignment with your highest good.

Your 'Go Word' Practice

One way to safeguard yourself is to choose a **"Go Word"** — a phrase that signals to Spirit, *"Yes, I'm ready now."*
This acts like a spiritual key, confirming which thoughts are serious and which are not.

Examples of Go Words:

- *"Activate."*
- *"Aligned now."*
- *"For my highest good."*
- *"Make it so."*

Choose one word or phrase that feels natural to you, and use it only when you are clear, focused, and ready. This tells Spirit that the desire has moved beyond a passing drift and into intentional creation.

The Safety Clause

Always pair your Go Word with the safeguard:
"...for my highest good and the highest good of all."

This ensures that even if your desire manifests quickly, it will do so in a way that uplifts and protects you.

This gives you both empowerment (*you're getting stronger at this*) and safety (*you won't accidentally manifest chaos*).

DAILY GO WORD RITUAL

1. **Center Yourself (1–2 minutes)**
   o Close your eyes. Take three deep breaths.
   o Place a hand over your heart and feel your body relax.
2. **Drift & Recognize**
   o Notice any thoughts or desires drifting through your mind.
   o Choose just one that feels aligned, clear, and important.
3. **Confirm Readiness**
   Ask yourself:
   o Am I willing to take action toward this?
   o Am I ready to receive this if it arrives sooner than expected?
   o Does this serve my highest good and the highest good of all?

   If the answer is yes, proceed. If not, gently release the thought.

4. **Speak Your Go Word**
   o Say your chosen word or phrase aloud (or silently with full intent).
   o Example: *"Activate, for my highest good and the highest good of all."*
   o Imagine your desire surrounded in light, sent forward with love and certainty.

5. **Seal with Gratitude**
    - ○ Whisper: *"Thank you, Spirit. I am ready."*
    - ○ Take one small aligned action today to show you mean it.

Tip: Practice this daily, even with small desires (finding a parking spot, a calm conversation, a joyful moment). It trains your mind and Spirit to know when you're serious — and helps prevent stray thoughts from manifesting unintentionally.

Appendix

The DREAM Method

D – Drift (Unconscious Thought: the spark, the first glimpse)
Every manifestation begins as a passing drift of thought. These "drift-thoughts" float through the mind almost unnoticed — subtle, fleeting, yet full of potential. Though you may not pay attention, Spirit hears them all.

R – Recognize (bringing unconscious into consciousness)
When you choose to notice and hold a thought, you bring it into focus. Recognition turns random sparks into intentional seeds. This is where you clarify and commit.

E – Execute (aligned action, practical and decisive)
Dreams need energy. Taking small, aligned steps — writing it down, speaking it, preparing for it — tells Spirit and your subconscious: *"I am serious."* Execution is the bridge from mind to matter.

A – Achieve (Manifest: live it)
The desire materializes. You step into the experience of what you once only imagined. This is the moment where thought becomes reality — the fruit of alignment, action, and Spirit's partnership.

M – Master (Evolve: reflect, refine, and repeat)
Every manifestation brings wisdom. Mastery means reflecting on what worked, what didn't, and how it shaped you. With

mastery, you evolve — ready to dream again, even bigger, even clearer.

Tagline: *Live the DREAM: Drift, Recognize, Execute, Achieve, Master.*

How to Write Affirmations

Affirmations are short, powerful statements that align your thoughts with your desires. They are the language you use to speak to your subconscious mind — and to Spirit. When written correctly, affirmations program your mind to believe, prepare, and act as though your manifestation is already true.

Guidelines for Writing Affirmations

1. **Write in the Present Tense**
   Affirmations should be stated as if they are already happening.

   - Instead of: *"I will be healthy."*
   - Say: *"I am healthy and full of energy."*

2. **Keep It Positive**
   Focus on what you want, not what you don't.

   - Instead of: *"I am not stressed."*
   - Say: *"I am calm, balanced, and at peace."*

3. **Make It Specific and Clear**
   The clearer your affirmation, the easier it is for your subconscious (and Spirit) to understand.

   - Instead of: *"I want money."*
   - Say: *"I easily attract $5,000 in new income opportunities."*

4. **Add Emotion**
   Feelings give affirmations power. Use words that stir excitement, gratitude, or joy.

   - Example: *"I am deeply grateful for the loving relationships in my life."*

5. **Keep It Believable**
   Affirmations must stretch you but still feel possible. If your subconscious rejects it, reframe it.

   - Instead of: *"I am a billionaire."* (if that feels too far away)
   - Try: *"I am consistently attracting opportunities that grow my wealth."*

6. **Start With "I Am" Statements**
   "I am" is one of the most powerful phrases in manifestation because it declares identity.

   - Example: *"I am worthy of love and success."*

7. **Repeat Often**
   Consistency rewires your brain. Write your affirmations, speak them out loud, and repeat them daily — ideally in the morning, before bed, or anytime you feel doubt creeping in.

Examples of Well-Written Affirmations

- *"I am living in a beautiful, safe home that supports my well-being."*
- *"I am surrounded by supportive friends who uplift and inspire me."*
- *"I am healthy, vibrant, and filled with abundant energy every day."*
- *"I am confidently stepping into my dream career."*

- *"I am grateful for the steady flow of money that supports my life and goals."*

Key Insight: Affirmations are not empty words. They are commands spoken with clarity, emotion, and intention — bridging unconscious thought into conscious creation.

D — Drift (Unconscious Thought)

- I welcome gentle, helpful thoughts to drift into my awareness.
- The seeds of my good arrive easily, even when I'm not looking.
- I am open to subtle whispers from Spirit and my subconscious.
- What is meant for me finds me—softly, clearly, repeatedly.
- I notice recurring nudges and honor them with curiosity.
- Inspiration visits me in perfect timing.

R — Recognize (Conscious Focus)

- I choose my focus with clarity and calm.
- I recognize what matters and release what doesn't.
- My intention is clear, simple, and strong.
- I hold my vision steadily and kindly.
- I give my chosen thought my loving attention.
- Clarity grows as I focus.

E — Execute (Aligned Action)

- I take one aligned step today.
- Small actions compound into big results for me.
- My calendar reflects my intentions.
- I move with purpose, grace, and momentum.
- Spirit meets me in motion.
- Doing a little now opens many doors later.

A — Achieve (Manifest / Live It)

- I allow good results to land and stay.
- I receive with gratitude and ease.
- Evidence of success shows up for me every day.
- I am living inside the reality I once imagined.
- My wins are real, and I celebrate them.
- What I envisioned is now experienced.

M — Master (Reflect, Refine, Repeat)

- I learn quickly and kindly from every outcome.
- Reflection refines me; wisdom guides me.
- I release what's not aligned and keep what is.
- Each cycle makes me clearer, stronger, freer.
- I begin again with deeper mastery.
- I live the DREAM—again and again.

One-Line Chain (use anytime)

I notice (Drift), choose (Recognize), move (Execute), receive (Achieve), and refine (Master).

Quick Goal Variations (optional)

- **Wealth:** I focus on value, act with discipline, and receive increasing income with gratitude.
- **Health:** I choose nourishing actions and feel vitality growing within me.
- **Love:** I lead with openness and let love arrive in kind, healthy ways.
- **Home/Car/Trip:** I take the next practical step and enjoy the experience as it becomes real.

Morning & Evening Cue

- **Morning:** *Today I live the DREAM—one clear focus, one aligned action.*
- **Evening:** *I honor today's progress and refine tomorrow with wisdom.*

Bibliography

Ariely, Dan. *Predictably Irrational: The Hidden Forces That Shape Our Decisions.* Harper Perennial, 2010.

Dispenza, Joe. *Breaking the Habit of Being Yourself: How to Lose Your Mind and Create a New One.* Hay House, 2012.

Dyer, Wayne. *The Power of Intention: Learning to Co-create Your World Your Way.* Hay House, 2004.

Frankl, Viktor E. *Man's Search for Meaning.* Beacon Press, 2006.

Freud, Sigmund. *The Interpretation of Dreams.* Basic Books, 2010 (originally published 1899).

James, William. *The Varieties of Religious Experience.* Penguin Classics, 1985 (originally published 1902).

Jung, Carl G. *Dreams.* Routledge, 2014.

Lipton, Bruce H. *The Biology of Belief: Unleashing the Power of Consciousness, Matter & Miracles.* Hay House, 2016.

Loftus, Elizabeth, and Katherine Ketcham. *The Myth of Repressed Memory: False Memories and Allegations of Sexual Abuse.* St. Martin's Press, 1996.

Murphy, Joseph. *The Power of Your Subconscious Mind.* TarcherPerigee, 2008 (originally published 1963).

Peale, Norman Vincent. *The Power of Positive Thinking.* Fireside, 2003 (originally published 1952).

Santego, Constance. *Fairy Tales, Dreams and Reality… Where Are You on Your Path?* Maximillian Enterprises, 2011.

Seligman, Martin E. P. *Authentic Happiness: Using the New Positive Psychology to Realize Your Potential for Lasting Fulfillment.* Atria Books, 2004.

Tolle, Eckhart. *The Power of Now: A Guide to Spiritual Enlightenment.* New World Library, 1999.

Vogt, Mark E. *Neuroscience and Consciousness: Exploring the Mind-Brain Relationship.* Academic Press, 2019.

Message From The Author

As you close the final pages of this book, I want to leave you with this reminder: manifestation is not reserved for the gifted few. It is not magic, luck, or chance. It is a living process, woven into the way thoughts become things, and dreams become reality. You are already manifesting every day — the difference now is that you hold the map.

The DREAM Method was born from decades of teaching, writing, and witnessing transformation. I've seen students and clients shift their lives in ways they once thought impossible. And I've lived this work myself, through struggles, breakthroughs, and faith in the unseen. That is why I know this: if you commit to the process, your life can and will change.

Remember, each step is simple, but none are small. Drift opens the door. Recognize gives you choice. Execute puts you in motion. Achieve lets you live the reality. Master transforms every experience into wisdom. And then, you begin again — clearer, stronger, more aligned.

So keep dreaming. Keep practicing. Keep stepping into the life that Spirit is always ready to co-create with you.

With gratitude and faith in your journey,
Dr. Constance Santego

Live the DREAM: Drift, Recognize, Execute, Achieve, Master.

About the Author

Dr. Constance Santego, Ph.D., DNM is a teacher, author, and visionary dedicated to bridging the gap between science, spirit, and self-empowerment. With over two decades of experience in health sciences, holistic wellness, energy medicine, and esthetics education, she has guided thousands of students worldwide to unlock their potential and step into lives of greater balance, purpose, and abundance.

As the author of more than forty books across both fiction and nonfiction, Dr. Santego has explored topics ranging from Reiki and intuitive development to energy medicine, personal growth, and spiritual transformation. Her work reflects her belief that true healing and manifestation begin with awareness — when the mind, body, and spirit align, transformation naturally follows.

Her signature **DREAM Method** (Drift, Recognize, Execute, Achieve, Master) was developed to make manifestation practical, repeatable, and deeply personal. Through her books, courses, and global workshops, she teaches that manifestation is not magic, but a natural process available to everyone — once they understand how thoughts evolve into reality.

When she is not teaching or writing, Dr. Santego continues her mission to empower others by mentoring entrepreneurs, creating transformative courses, and inspiring communities through her YouTube channel and speaking engagements. She lives in beautiful British Columbia, where she enjoys nature, family, and the everyday magic of living what she teaches.

ALSO AVAILABLE

For additional information on

Constance Santego's

wide range of Motivational Products, Coaching Sessions,
Spiritual Retreats,
Live Events and Educational Programs

Go to

www.ConstanceSantego.ca

Follow on Instagram - Constance_Santego and
Facebook - constancesantegoo

Subscribe and receive Free Information and Meditations
on her
YouTube Channel - Constance Santego

If you've studied with me before, you may recognize echoes of
what I taught in my *Fairy Tales, Dreams, and Reality* course
and *The Art of Manifestation*. This book is the evolution of
those teachings — updated, expanded, and reshaped into a
method that is both practical and profound. The DREAM
Method is the next step in a journey we have been on together,
designed to guide you more clearly than ever before.

Softcover: Available at **Barnes & Noble, Indigo/Chapters, and Amazon**
Soft Cover ISBN: 9781990062155